THE MEXICAN HISTORICAL
NOVEL

THE MEXICAN HISTORICAL NOVEL

1826—1910

By

J. LLOYD READ, PH. D.

Professor of Romance Languages in the
Southwest Texas State Teachers College
San Marcos, Texas

NEW YORK / RUSSELL & RUSSELL

FIRST PUBLISHED IN 1939 BY
INSTITUTO DE LAS ESPAÑAS EN LOS ESTADOS UNIDOS
REISSUED, 1973, BY RUSSELL & RUSSELL
A DIVISION OF ATHENEUM PUBLISHERS, INC.
BY ARRANGEMENT WITH
HISPANIC INSTITUTE, COLUMBIA UNIVERSITY, NEW YORK
L. C. CATALOG CARD NO: 72-85005
ISBN 0-8462-1688-4
PRINTED IN THE UNITED STATES OF AMERICA

TO MY WIFE

PREFACE

In this treatise the term historical novel is used to include prose fiction that attempts a vitalization and interpretation of characters, movements or conditions of epochs that are now past. The purposes of such fiction should not be confused with those of formal history. While the historian strives to reconstruct a period by sorting his factual materials into a complete record of men's significant actions and into an exposition of the development of social forces and institutions, the historical novelist aspires to bring new life into his characters, permitting them to move, to speak, to love, to hate, to feel again the passions of their day. His work is that of revitalization of both characters and their environment.

It will be apparent as this study progresses that the works involved fall naturally into two groups, the romantic historical novels that deal with the conquest period and colonial times, and the novels that deal with historical events of the nineteenth century.

The first group is essentially romantic, corresponding to the type developed by Walter Scott but with a distinctly local "middle ages". Instead of turning to medieval Europe for exotic material, Mexican writers of this type of fiction sought out characters and institutions of their own dim past. Their hostility to the Spanish regime was still fresh enough to inspire them with a feeling of spiritual kinship with the Amerinds who had been the traditional enemies of the Europeans. Mexico had begun to take pride in its Indianism. The Aztec eagle on the cactus bush, holding a serpent in its mouth, became the national emblem, and the Amerind leaders became the idealized subjects of poetic fancy, interpreted in a conventional manner.

In this same group of romantic historical novels belong those fictional works that deal with colonial times. The Inquisition, mysterious, austere and awe-inspiring, is naturally the center of interest of these poetic interpretations of life in the colony.

The second class of Mexican historical novels is that which finds its material in the history of the nineteenth century, the epoch in which the authors themselves lived. In some cases the writers themselves had been actors in the dramas they presented. Such works may properly be called novels of contemporary history. Many of them were patterned after the *Episodios nacionales* of Pérez Galdós and the various historical romances of Erckmann-Chatrian.

But though these two groups of works deal with materials from widely separated periods, they have much in common. Whatever the period involved, it was interpreted in terms of the ideals of the nineteenth century when Mexico was attempting to constitute itself a new nation and to adapt itself to the ideas of the nineteenth-century world. Patriotism, a new sense of national identity and zeal for liberty and justice were the emotive forces that determined the trend of

Preface

interpretation in both groups of historical novels to which attention has been called.

It is interesting to note that in Mexico historical fiction, though not acclaimed so enthusiastically as in Europe, has had a considerable following in every generation since its inception. Explanation for this sustained interest is probably to be found in the fact that ideals of liberty and justice, of which historical fiction has been one expression, have been constantly on the defensive in a grave struggle for survival. The sense of danger and the possibility of frustration of those ideals have served to keep them fresh and dynamic in the ideology of liberal factions and has developed the sort of loyalty that normally associates itself with a protracted struggle for principle.

It was with the hope of making available a study of this branch of the literature of Mexico that this treatise was undertaken. It was thought logical to present the authors in the order of the dates of publication of their respective first novels.

The writer wishes to express his gratitude to Dr. Federico de Onís of Columbia University for his advice in matters of criticism, and to Dr. Ángel del Río also of the Hispanic Section of Columbia University for his suggestions in matters of organization and form. To Dr. Carlos Castañeda of the University of Texas a debt of gratitude is acknowledged for his kindness in making available the Spanish-American Library of that institution.

CONTENTS

Contents

THE MEXICAN HISTORICAL
NOVEL

CHAPTER I

INTRODUCTION

A. THE CHRONICLES OF THE INDIES AS REMOTE ORIGINS OF THE MEXICAN HISTORICAL NOVEL

Literary interpretation of the facts of history has been an important phase of Spanish literature from its very inception. From the *cantares de gesta,* both in poetic form and in prosified versions, through the *Anales toledanos* of the first half of the thirteenth century and the *Crónica general* of the time of Alfonso the Sage, on through the *romances,* or ballads, the various chronicles of the fifteenth century, the novels of chivalry, the historical novels of the type of *Guerras civiles de Granada,* and through many important works of the Golden Age the thread of historical material runs in almost unbroken continuity. Prominent in much of this literature is a remarkably successful attempt at synthesis of the soul of Spain, a blending of the facts of history into an artistic expression of the spiritual constitution of the race. Through it all there is in constant evidence a preoccupation with the greatness and dignity of racial role and of individual character.

1

Such literature received new impetus with the discovery of the new world. Indeed the facts relative thereto furnished an appeal and inspiration that history had never before offered the writer. Pedro Mártir de Anglería expressed an universal reaction when he wrote to Pomponio Leto:

> ... ¿qué mejor manjar puede presentarse a los grandes ingenios? ¿Qué convite más agradable? De mí sé decir que ... siento ... un gozo inefable. Gócense los miserables con la idea de acumular inmensos tesoros; los viciosos con los placeres; mientras nosotros, elevando nuestra mente a la contemplación divina, admiramos su inagotable poder, y recreamos nuestros ánimos con la noticia y conocimiento de cosas tan inauditas y singulares.[1]

The many accounts of the discovery and conquest may roughly be considered collectively a new heroic literature; new, however, only be-

---

[1]Enrique de Vedia: *Historiadores primitivos de Indias,* in *Biblioteca de Autores Españoles,* Madrid, 1918, Vol. 22, p. vi.

[... what better food could be given to great genius? What more agreeable feast? For my part ... I feel ... an ineffable pleasure. Let miserable souls take delight in the idea of amassing immense treasures and the vicious in pleasures, while we, raising our minds to divine contemplation, admire His (God's) power, and refresh our souls with the news and knowledge of such unheard-of and singular things.]

cause its subject matter is new, for its approach
is that of the older Spanish chronicles. Its re-
percussions were nevertheless broader than those
of any group of historical works previously
written. No branch of human learning escaped
its influence, least of all philosophy and literature. The horizons of thought were pushed back
to hazy distances. The knowledge that large
branches of the human family, previously un-
suspected, peopled vast expanses of territory,
likewise unimagined, aroused an intense interest
in humanity and in all phases of its life. That
interest was and is the most important food of
romantic literature. We have already called attention to its presence in early historico-literary
trends in Spain, and shall later see its importance in the branch of Mexican literature falling within the range of this study.

In most of this historical writing the typically
Spanish "ever present anxiety to select significant facts from experience and not to invent
apart from experience" is the significant characteristic.

Secular Prose Chronicles

The connection between the histories of Indian affairs and the historical literature of Mex-

ico is sufficiently close to justify a list of the best known of the former and the brief discussion of a few of them. At least the following should be listed:

Martín Fernández de Enciso: *Summa de geografía.*

Hernán Cortés: *Cartas de relación,* written between 1519 and 1526. Published in folios soon afterwards in Spain.

Pedro Mártir: *Decades de orbe novo,* Alcalá, 1530.

Gonzalo Fernández de Oviedo: *Historia general y natural de las Indias,* 1535, 1851-55.

Bartolomé de las Casas: *Historia general de las Indias,* and *Brevísima relación de la destrucción de las Indias,* 1552.

Bernal Díaz del Castillo: *Verdadera historia de la conquista de Nueva España,* 1568.

Francisco López de Gómara: *Historia general de las Indias,* 1552.

Francisco de Xérez: *Relación de la conquista del Perú,* 1534.

Agustín de Zárate: *Historia del Perú.* Author died after 1560.

Pedro Cieza: *La crónica del Perú,* 1553.

Francisco Cervantes de Salazar: *Crónica de la Nueva España.* Written before 1567, not published until 1914.

Pedro Simón: *Noticias historiales de la conquista de Tierra Firme en las Indias occidentales,* 1626 and 1892.

Fr- Bernardino de Sahagún: *Historia general de las cosas de Nueva España,* written 1569, published 1829-30.

Anon.: *Códice Ramírez,* written about the middle of the sixteenth century (?), discovered in Mexico in 1856, published in Mexico, 1878.

Ixtlilxóchitl: *Historia chichimeca.* Author died 1648. Work published by Kingsborough, 1848.

Hernando Alvarado Tezozomoc: *Crónica mexicana.* Written 1598 (?), published for first time by Kingsborough in 1848 as a part of his *Antiquities of Mexico.*

Garcilaso de la Vega (el inca): *Florida del Inca, Los comentarios reales* (1609?), and *Historia general del Perú.*

Pedro Aguado: *Historia de Santa María, y del nuevo reino de Granada,* and *Historia de Venezuela,* written in latter half of 16th century, published 1918.

Antonio de Solís: *Historia de la conquista de México*, 1684.

Clavigiero: *Historia antigua de México*, 1780-81.

The *Cartas de relación* of Hernan Cortés, the first extensive work on the New World, contain both materials and attitudes that are important as sources of the historical novel of Spanish America. No literary genius could have drawn from the realm of fancy a fabric more exotic and interesting than the bare facts with which Cortés dealt in a simple and forthright narrative and expository style. Critics have rightly called attention to the fact that his interests were broader and more human than those of Caesar in the latter's account of the conquest of Gaul. Caesar's interpretation of his conquest is a severely martial epic, the product of the Roman ideal of military might exercised for the glory and advantage of Rome. In keeping with much of the historico-literary traditions of Spain, Cortés' work is pointed primarily toward humanity, its interests and its institutions. The Indians were not only an enemy to be conquered, nor was the aim of the Spaniards purely military strategy. No individual nor any group of individuals assumes importance except as an agent of his own civilization. The individualism of the characters looms large, but is always in compatibility with their missionary role, never in divergence therefrom. This tendency to give effective characterization to an individual within the framework of institutional ideals will be recognized as proceeding from the spirit of antecedent historico-literary writings, and from continued obedience to principles that had guided the production of such works throughout their development. In the hands of capable writers and applied to inherently stirring materials its possibilities were great; but its use holds the danger of sterility in character portrayal in the hands of undisciplined members of a social community characterized by artistic immaturity. Of this fact abundant evidence is found in much of Mexico's literature based on history.

Enrique de Vedia calls attention to the dignity, modesty and simple effectiveness of Cortés' style.[1] By his evenness of tone and almost complete impersonalization of himself Cortés placed his work on a dignifed plane.

---

[1]*Ibid.*, p. xvii.

Few of his fellow chroniclers approached him in this regard.

Very little concerning the life of the Indians, the topography of the country explored and the vegetable and animal life escaped Cortés' attention. The physical appearance of the natives, their clothes and personal adornments, their food and its preparation, their domestic architecture, their social classes and the condition of each, their religious beliefs and ceremonies, their moral state and their customs, their products, their arts and their industry are dwelt on at length and frequently.

In his comments on the aborigines Cortés revealed the strong crusading spirit to which attention has already been called. He is not an intrepid warrior bent on conquest as an end in itself, but rather one who confused his own glory with loyalty to his ideals, some of which were worldly and some almost mystic. In his first letter to his king he wrote:

> Podrán vuestras majestades, si fueran servidos, hacer por verdadera relación a nuestro muy santo Padre para que en la conversión desta gente se ponga diligencia y buena orden . . . y evitarán (los indios) tan grandes males y daños como son los que en el servicio del diablo hacen . . . En todo suplicamos a vuestras majestades manden proveer

como vieren que más conviene al servicio de Dios
y de vuestras reales altezas, y como los que en su servicio aquí estamos, seamos favorecidos y aprove-
chados.[1]

Repeatedly he expressed compassion for the
conquered. And though we have no interest in
making out a brief in defense of his alleged
greed and lust for glory, it is important that at
least these motives were sublimated by fusion
with mystic motives. That process is common
in much of the writing on the Indies. It is a
literary device used extensively by colonial writers and by historical novelists of the nineteenth
century in Mexico.

From the standpoint of romantic interest not
even *Robinson Crusoe* has more appeal than some
parts of Cortés' account. The facts with which
the latter dealt were more multitudinous and less

---

[1]*Ibid.*, p. 10.

[Your royal majesties may, if they so desire, in-
form our most holy Father of this, so that the conversion of this people may be undertaken with dili-
gence and good order . . . and they (the Amerinds)
will be delivered from the great evils and harmful
practices such as they give themselves to in the
service of the devil . . . In everything we pray
that your royal majesties make provision for all
that is needed in the service of God and of your
royal majesties and that those of us who are in the
service here may be favored and upheld.]

closely tied on to a central theme than the imagined happenings of Defoe's work, but were no less exotic and stirring. Novelists who later attempted fiction based on the conquest and on Indian life of the preconquest period drew heavily on Cortés both for materials and for exotic tone.

Few indeed were these novelists, especially those of liberal leanings, that did not also use the *Historia de Indias* and the *Brevísima relación de la destrucción de las Indias* of Bartolomé de las Casas. His decided sympathy for the Indians and his attacks on the Europeans were almost made to order for their artistic as well as political purposes. Anticipating Rousseau and Voltaire by centuries, this venerable priest idealized the aborigines until they became to him the noble innocent savage, victim of the avarice and corruption of civilization. No other theme could have appealed more to the liberal element of nineteenth-century Mexico, which in its enthusiasm for its new-found liberty, was naturally striving to escape from the old horizons of its inherited civilization and to see with sympathy every force that had ever opposed that order. Whether Hurtado's opinion that Casas ". . . hid his literary and political incapacity under a cloak of rancid preoccupations . . ."[1] is true or not, it is certain that his attitude gave encouragement to the cult of the primitive in human society. The school of romanticism fed eagerly on a source so definitely to its liking.

Gómara's statement, "Comenzaron las conquistas de indios acabada la de moros, porque siempre guerreasen españoles contra infieles,"[2] reveals his conviction that Spain was fulfilling a predestined role. His *Historia general de las Indias* carries the same tone throughout. The dominance of this attitude has been sufficiently emphasized in dealing with the older chronicles to justify lack of further comment here.

But Gómara's serious preoccupations did not drive him to asceticism and disdain for the beauties of this world. His senses were keenly awake to the attractions of the physical universe around him. His *Historia general de las Indias* begins:

---

[1]Hurtado y Palencia: *Historia de la literatura española,* Madrid, 1925, p. 431.

[2]Francisco López de Gómara: *Historia general de las Indias, Biblioteca de Autores Españoles,* Vol. 22, p. 156.

[When the conquest of the Moors was over that of the Indians began so that Spaniards might always fight infidels.]

Es el mundo tan grande y hermoso, y tiene
tanta diversidad de cosas tan diferentes unas de
otras, que pone admiración a quien bien lo piensa
y contempla. Pocos hombres hay, si ya no viven
como brutos animales, que no se pongan alguna
vez a considerar sus maravillas, porque natural es
a cada uno el deseo de saber.[1]

The procedure of Gómara, more frankly literary than that of Cortés, brings into bolder relief the interest in humanity of a type unknown
to Europeans and in the more human emotions
of the conquerors.

A great deal of space is devoted to description of the Indians, their customs, their food,
their products and their mental and spiritual
traits. More than any previous writer of treatises
on New World affairs, Gómara called on the
instruments of literary art. He approached more
nearly the imaginative interpretation of Ercilla
than any of his predecessors had done. His work
represents an advance toward prose historical
fiction in this regard.

---

[1]Enrique de Vedia: *op. cit.*, Vol. 22, p. 157.

[The earth is so great and beautiful, and it has
such great diversity of things so different each from
the others, that one who thinks and contemplates
is struck with admiration. Few men there are indeed, if they do not live like dumb animals, who do
not sometimes ponder its marvels, because it is the
nature of man to strive to know.]

An interesting trend in Gómara's work, as well as in that of most of the better known chroniclers of Indian affairs, is the refusal to indulge in empty peroration. The taint of inflated rhetoric is fortunately absent throughout. His was a serious art, too weighty for artificial decoration. His literary effectiveness is attained within the bounds of realistic procedure, heightened only by an attractive simplicity of style and good judgment. His moderation imparts a tone of dignity and artistic integrity. But with all his good judgment and moderation Gómara reaches heights of interest untouched by the best products of the unrestrained fancy of the romances of chivalry. The alleged idealization of Cortés as his main character is not a departure from reality, but merely a matter of relative emphasis, a more profound reality than any recital of bare facts could be.

Bernal Díaz del Castillo, in a style characteristic of a man of action without literary training, related the happenings connected with the conquest as an eye-witness. Without concern for the demands of either history or literature he incorporated both in his direct sincere story. To the extent that fiction should include naturalness, emphasis on picturesque details, interest in human nature, appreciation of personal courage and of nature in all of its aspects, Mexican historical fiction must count Díaz del Castillo as one of its precursors.

The *Sumario de la natural historia de las Indias* of Hernández de Oviedo y Valdés is, as the title indicates, a treatise on the aspects of physical nature, the ethnology of the Indians, the flora and fauna of the New World. Though its materials might have been used with good results by later historical novelists they were not utilized to any considerable extent. Since its aim was largely scientific, its literary influence was not great.

With the intention of giving his king information concerning the "admirable things" to be found in Peru, the majestic mountains, valleys, rivers, diverse peoples and their customs, animal and vegetable life that served as a setting for the equally strange deeds of the Spanish conquerors, Pedro de Cieza de León wrote *La crónica del Perú*. His question

Sin lo cual, ¿quién podrá contar los nunca oídos trabajos que tan pocos españoles en tanta grandeza de tierra han pasado?[1]

[1]*Ibid.*, Vol. 26, p. 349.

[Without which (referring to the natural set-

and his emphasis on the personal experiences of
the actors, "hunger, thirst, death, fears and exhaustion," indicate his interest in the subjective
possibilities of his theme. There appears an occasional note of drama in the fight of men
against the obstacles imposed by nature, a theme
pregnant with literary possibilities. There stand
out alternately a compassion for the Amerinds
in their subjection to injustice, and condemnation of their savage customs. Nature, white men
and primitive Amerinds are like sides of a tri-
angle around which the author traveled as he
wrote. His work is for the most part a series of
creative descriptions of various settlements in an
exotic background. His interests were not those
of the historian intent on objective presentation,
but those of an individual who gave play to his
subjective reactions, a fact that augments the
work's literary value to the same degree that it
lessens its historical accuracy. For its naturalness, its apparent sincerity, its good taste and
its genuinely exotic materials it is important
as a literary force.

---

ting), who would ever be able to relate the works
that so few Spaniards in such a great part of the
earth have done?]

Garcilaso de la Vega, the Inca, incorporated into his work the products of the mental genius of his mother's race. Richness of imagination and emotional resources and unpretentious simplicity lend an air of creative literature to his accounts of New World affairs. The legends of his Inca kinsmen, woven into the body of his works, constitute historical fiction of unquestionable value, both intrinsically and from the standpoint of development of the genre.

Garcilaso selected the striking phases of his people's traditions and of the conquest. Without the sound criteria necessary for history, he put into his compositions whatever appealed to his fancy. Therein lies his importance as a source of historical fiction. His essentially romantic interests led him to emphasize the picturesque, the legendary, the exotic, and to esteem more highly the interest of his story than the formal demands of composition. Unity is often lacking because of the author's habit of interpolating material whose only justification is its inherent interest. Here indeed was a romanticist in the making.

One example of Garcilaso's interest in historical fiction is his treatment of the story of Pedro

Serrano in his *Comentarios reales*. Serrano was shipwrecked while making a voyage from Cartagena to Havana. Clinging to floating wreckage, he was cast on an uninhabited island bare of water and vegetation. His only food was the flesh of sea turtles and other creatures that lived in the water, and his only drink was the rain water he caught and the blood of the turtles he ate.

After several years of solitary life on his island, Serrano came upon a stranger. The reciprocal fear of the two led them to call upon the Christian saints for protection. When each saw that the other was of Christian faith their fears vanished and they became friends. Four years passed before a passing ship bore them away from the island.

There are few plot elements in *Robinson Crusoe* whose seeds are not found in this story. The framework for Garcilaso's plot was not original, however, since it was based on a true episode; but his treatment and interpretation of it are sufficiently original to make of it a bit of true fiction.

But for all the affinity of Garcilaso for the interesting and striking, his works reveal with

accuracy the true spirit of the times with which
he dealt, and are in the main in conformity with
the facts of history. It is this conformity to facts
that keeps him from being a true historical
novelist.

Of great importance to the group of novelists
that attempted to give artistic resurrection to the
peoples that inhabited the New World before the
European intrusion were the anonymous *Códice
Ramírez* (about the middle of the sixteenth century?), so-called because it was discovered by
José Fernando Ramírez, the *Historia chichimeca*
of Ixtlilxóchitl (1568?-1648), the works of Garcilaso de la Vega, already discussed, and the
Crónica mexicana (1598?) of Hernando de Alvarado Tezozomoc. All these works contain a
great deal of legendary material gathered from
natives taught while young to recite their race's
traditions, from popular versions of the remote
past, from fragmentary records in hieroglyphics,
and from the scattered remnants of the higher
native classes. Ixtlilxóchitl dealt with the Tex-
cocans, Tezozomoc with the Aztecs and Garcilaso
with the Incas. The very difficulty of these men
as historians, namely the vagueness and remote-
ness of their material, was their literary op-

portunity. The poetic haze of distance was ready-made.

The *Códice Ramírez,* discovered by José F. Ramírez in 1856 and edited for the first time in 1878, is one of the most valuable works on the history of the Amerinds of Mexico. From the origin of the inhabitants of the country, shrouded in the mists of antiquity, the author, himself a native, traced the wanderings of the various tribes and the development of their civilizations according to their traditions. The author's point of view was clearly not that of a Spanish historian attempting to write the history of tribes that to him were heathen, but that of a member of a race that had seen its glory disappear before the superior military might of European invaders. The soul of the Amerind child of nature, following implicitly the will of the gods that inhabited idols and the physical aspects of nature, pervades the entire work. The Jewish scriptures contain no more consciousness of divine leadership and of a promised land nor more foreboding of periodic tribulations and ultimate destruction than does this work. Far from being a history of actions, it is the history of the soul of a people still simple and natural enough to hear the voice of the Creator in the winds, the waters and the hills, and to attribute every turn of fortune to His inexorable and inscrutable will. A short summary of one episode will reveal much of the spirit of the work.

Motecuczuma, the Aztec king, ordered an army of workmen to bring to his capital a great stone, that he might offer a worthy sacrifice to the Aztec god. The stone refused to be moved and cried out to the workmen that such a sacrifice was against the will of the Creator. When they persisted in their attempts the stone disappeared into the ground.

An Indian laborer sowing his fields was, at about the same time, seized by an eagle and transported without harm to a cavern where Motecuczuma was sleeping, heedless of the suffering of his people and unmindful of the calamities that the gods had decreed for him as punishment for his crimes and pride. An unseen spokesman revealed the fate of the sleeping king to the laborer, then commanded the eagle to return the latter to his fields.

The next day the Indian reported the matter to the king. Thereafter for a year a strange cloud of flame appeared in the sky as a warning of dire things to come. A great flame came out of the forests and enveloped the city. Water poured on the fire merely increased its ravages. A comet with three heads blazed across the sky at midday filling the heavens with sparks, and the lake that separated Mexico from Tetzcuco boiled for no apparent reason and overflowed parts of the city. At night there was heard from the sky the strange voice of a woman wailing in anguish over the approaching destruction of her people.

A group of fishermen captured a strange bird and took it to Motecuczuma. In the middle of its head it had a strange mirror which even at noon reflected the sky with all of its stars. In this mirror Motecuczuma saw approaching from the east a band of strange warriors. Before the wise men could explain the riddle, the bird disappeared. At this juncture came news of the arrival of ships bearing strange men off the coast of Vera Cruz. The series of dire events foretold had begun to come to pass.

It is little wonder that a work so rich in literary material should appeal to novelists of the nineteenth century. But that material did not reach them directly through the *Códice Ramírez* until 1878. It had been available before that date, however, in Durán's *Historia de las Indias de Nueva España y islas de Tierra Firme,* (1867), in José de Acosta's *Historia natural y moral de las Indias* (1590), and in Alva Ixtlilxóchitl's *Historia chichimeca,* published by Lord Kingsborough in his *Antiquities of Mexico* in 1848. All of these works borrowed some of their materials from the *Códice Ramírez.*

Alva Ixtlilxóchitl's work, composed of the five *Relaciones de los tultecas,* eleven parts of the *Historia de los señores chichimecas,* the *Ordenanzas de Nezahualcoyotl,* thirteen *Relaciones de la noticia de los pobladores,* the *Relaciones sucinta y sumaria,* the *Historia chichimeca,* and various known fragments, was based on hieroglyphic paintings that furnished the chronology and the outstanding events of the history of the tribes concerned, on old heroic compositions that supplied details and color, and on the testimony of witnesses that had survived the destruction of official records.

In the dedicatory note of *Historia chichimeca* the author asserts his conviction that the events of the history of the Amerinds were as interesting and important as those of the history of the

Romans, the Greeks and other non-Christian peoples of the world. Beginning with the story of the creation of the world the author took up the history of his people from remote antiquity.

Whatever may be said of the historical accuracy of Ixtlilxóchitl's work, its interest is unquestionable. Fortunately, from a literary standpoint, he relied partly on the poetical traditions of the Amerinds for his material. His sense of the picturesque, his grace and often eloquent language give his works a literary value that is coming to be recognized as significant.

Much of the material of Ixtlilxóchitl's work as well as that of several of the other historians of Amerind affairs came to Mexican readers in Prescott's fascinating *The Conquest of Mexico*, of which there were two translations in 1844, one published by I. Cumplido and the other by V. García Torres.

Chronicles of Religious Orders

There was another type of records of affairs in New Spain that cannot be overlooked. The various religious orders kept chronicles of events affecting their members during colonization and the conversion of the natives. The material found in such records is part history and

part sacred epic in prose, following in general
the same trend as the histories of saints and religious orders prominent in Spain from an early
date. Such a work is *Historia del Nayarit, Sonora, Sinaloa y ambas Californias* of José de Ortega, published first in Barcelona in 1754 with
the title of *Apostólicos afanes de la Compañía de
Jesús en la América septentrional* and again in
Mexico in 1887 under the first title mentioned
above with a prologue written by Manuel de Ola-
guibel.

The work is an interesting history in narrative
form of the struggles of Jesuit priests to explore
the territories of Sonora, Sinaloa and the Californias, and to Christianize the barbarous inhabitants. The topography of the region and the customs of the savages are dwelt on, not because the
author realized their literary value, but because
the former heightened the sense of difficulty under which the fathers worked and the latter furnished a system by comparison with which Christianity is seen in a favorable light, a system in
whose destruction the Jesuits proved their zeal for
the faith and their service to humanity. The result
is not greatly changed by the motives of the author, however, and the exotic element is one of the

work's greatest attractions. Indeed the Amerinds in their mountain fastnesses, fighting invaders much better equipped than they, come near to being the chief attraction.

Chronicles in Verse

The epic nature of the conquest found expression also in verse. At the same time that Herrera "el Divino" was writing his patriotic odes on affairs of the homeland, Alonso de Ercilla was publishing his *La Araucana,* an heroic poem of thirty-seven cantos based on the struggle of the Araucanian Indians of Chile to defend their independence against the invading Spaniards. More than any other account of the conquest so far discussed *La Araucana* approaches true literary creation and interpretation of its historical materials. It comes near to furnishing the last step in the development of a true literature based on history, namely, the animation through creative imagination of the scenes, characters and action; but it lacks freedom from the tyranny of historical facts in its general outline, a defect that few Mexican historical novelists were capable of escaping later on.

This defect arose from the author's confessed purpose of writing history. Internal evidence proves that Ercilla knew the demands as well as the delights of true epic poetry, but his purpose was not to follow them. Within his self-imposed limitations, however, he succeeded in breathing life into his work.

More than any of the other authors discussed in this introduction, Ercilla used the moods of nature to give beauty and dramatic effect to his account. In his work, too, the Indian assumes a more heroic nature. In Bartolomé de las Casas' writings the Indian was child-like and innocent, but in *La Araucana* he was strong and courageous, an enemy worthy of the Spaniard.

> Este es el fiero pueblo no domado,
> .   .   .   .
> y puso al español en tal aprieto.[1]
>
> Vienen a ser tan sueltos y alentados
> Que alcanzan por aliento los venados.[2]
>
> Del escuadrón se van adelantando
> Los bárbaros que son sobresalientes,

---

[1] Alonso de Ercilla: *La Araucana*, Madrid, Imp. Nacional, 1866, vol. 1, p. 12.

[This is the fierce people never conquered
.   .   .   .
And (who) put the Spaniards in such difficulties.]
[2] *Ibid.*, p. 13.
[They come to be so agile and so untiring
That they run down deer by their endurance.]

> Soberbios cielo y tierra despreciando,
> Ganosos de estremarse por valientes.[1]

It is strange that Mexican writers of historical fiction did not develop the possibilities of Ercilla's example in this heroic treatment of the Indian. Few of them did more than make of him a sentimental child of nature, victim of the white man.

Ercilla continued the moral and philosophical tone to which attention has been called and which was prevalent in Mexico's historical fiction. For example:

> No entienden con la próspera bonanza
> Que el contento es principio de tristeza.
>
> . . . .
>
> Que en el fin de la vida está la prueba
>
> . . . .
>
> El más seguro bien de la fortuna
> Es no haberla tenido vez alguna.[2]

---

[1]*Ibid.*, p. 15.
[Of the squadron there come advancing
Barbarians of unusual prowess,
Defying proudly both heaven and earth
Desiring to excel by extremes of bravery.]
[2]*Ibid.*, pp. 28-29.
[Men do not understand in prosperity
That contentment is the first stage of sadness

. . . .

That the proof of life is in its end

. . . .

> ¡Oh incurable mal! ¡o gran fatiga![1]
> ¡Oh insaciable codicia de mortales![2]

Juan de Castellanos' treatment of historical material in *Elegías de varones ilustres de Indias* is described in his own words:

> Ni cantaré fingidos beneficios
> De Prometeo, hijo de Japeto,
> Fantaseando vanos edificios
> Con harto más estima que el efeto;
> Como los que con grandes artificios
> Van supliendo las faltas del sujeto;
> Porque las grandes cosas que yo digo
> Su punto y su valor tienen consigo.[3]

B. GENERAL TRENDS OF MEXICAN LITERATURE PRIOR TO
   AND CONTEMPORARY WITH THE APPEARANCE OF
   THE HISTORICAL NOVEL

Immediately after the completion of the conquest, there began a movement to transplant to

---

The surest good of fortune
Is never to have had it.]

[1]*Ibid.*, p. 52.

[Oh incurable ill! Oh great fatigue!]

[2]*Ibid.*, p. 52.

[Oh insatiable greed of mortals!]

[3]Juan de Castellanos: *Elegías de varones ilustres de Indias* in *Biblioteca de Autores Españoles*, Vol. IV, p. 5.

[I shall not sing feigned benefits
Of Prometheus, son of Iapetus,
In fancy building vain structures
With values more imagined than real,
Like those who with great skill

the colony the civilization of the mother country. The greatest problem involved in this task was the conversion and education of the natives. Schools for the Indians were accordingly opened almost as soon as the sound of clashing arms had died away. Fray Pedro de Gante, landing in New Spain in 1523, founded the *Colegio de San Francisco de México*, the first educational institution of the New World; in 1536 the *Colegio de Santa Cruz de Tlaltelolco* was founded to provide instruction beyond the elementary level for the natives; the *Colegio de San Juan Letrán* was founded soon afterwards for the *mestizos* or half-breeds. Under the direction of the various religious orders other schools sprang up in rapid succession. The Jesuits extended their territory by establishing branches of the *Colegio Máximo* in almost every large city of the colony. In 1553 the *Universidad de México* was opened. It is eloquent testimony to the vigor and enthusiasm of the leaders of the educational movement that less than thirty-five years after the forces of Cortés marched into Mexico City a university

---

Correct the faults of their subjects;
Because the great things of which I write
Have their interest and their value inherent in
  them.]

was in operation with a faculty comparable in many ways to the faculties of European universities.

In 1536 a printing press was set up in Mexico City. By 1579 there were four in the capital. These presses became valuable aids in the dissemination of Spanish culture in the colony.

The literature of Mexico during the colonial period was naturally a reflection of Spanish literature. The institutions of higher learning, patterned after those of Spain, were manned by neo-scholastic scientists and peripatetic philosophers, by learned rhetoricians and humanistic scholars trained in Spain, France and Italy. The constant coming and going of Spaniards of all types kept the colony in touch with affairs in Spain.

A perusal of the bibliography of the sixteenth century in New Spain reveals the fact that attention was centered on four fields: doctrine, native linguistics, secular chronicles and the chronicles of the religious orders. There was no fiction, no drama of importance, and little worthwhile poetry, though González de Eslava has one of his characters say: " . . . hay más

poetas que estiércol."[1] The only prose work
that can lay claim to literary amenity is the *Diá-
logos* of Cervantes Salazar appended to a critical edition of Juan Luis Vives' work of the same
name.[2] Its main interest lies in its descriptions
of Mexico City and the surrounding territory.

In poetry New Spain followed, at least in
form, the trends of the Golden Age of Spanish
literature. The outstanding production of the
century was the poem *La grandeza mexicana* of
Bernardo de Balbuena, published in 1604, in
which the author attempted to paint the grandeur of the colony and its inhabitants.

In fragments of other poems that have been
preserved there is evidence that many poets engaged in the attempt to create an epic poetry
based on the conquest; but little worthy of remark was attained.

More important for our purposes than the artistic value of the verse and prose of the early
days of New Spain is a note of social discord
that became audible therein, namely, the con-

---

[1] Quoted in González Peña: *op. cit.*, p. 84.

[2] Francisco Cervantes de Salazar: *Obras que Francisco Cervantes de Salazar ha hecho, glosado y traducido,* Alcalá de los Henares, Juan de Brocar, 1546.

flict between the Spaniard and the creole that
has colored so much of Mexico's social life and
literature. Dorantes de Carranza declaimed:

> ¡Oh Indias! madre de extraños, abrigo de foragi-
> dos y delincuentes, patria común a los innaturales,
> dulce beso y de paz a los recién venidos.[1]

Terrazas decried the same injustices thus:

> Madrastra nos has sido rigurosa y dulce madre
> pía a los extraños. . .[2]

and a well known sonnet expresses a similar
complaint thus:

> Viene de España por el mar salobre
> a nuestro mexicano domicilio
> Un hombre tosco sin algún auxilio,
> De salud falto y de dinero pobre.
>
> Y luego que caudal y ánimo cobra,
> Le aplican en su bárbaro concilio,
> Otros como él, de César y Virgilio
> Las dos coronas de laurel y robre.
> Y el otro que agujetas y alfileres
> Vendía por las calles, ya es un conde
> En calidad y en cantidad un Fúcar:
>
> Y abomina después el lugar donde

---

[1]González Peña: *op. cit.*, p. 105.

[Oh Indies! Mother to strangers, shelter of vil-
lians and delinquents, common fatherland of the
unnatural, sweet kiss of peace to new arrivals.]

[2]*Ibid.*, p. 105.

[A harsh stepmother have you been to us and
sweet pious mother to strangers.]

Adquirió estimación, gusto y haberes,
Y tiraba la jábega en Sanlúcar.[1]

Here began in Mexican literature the treatment
of the cleavage between the two principal groups
of society, a cleavage that burdens many of the
novels of the nineteenth century.

Almost all types of compositions in New
Spain in the seventeenth century fell ready prey
to the infection of Gorgorism. Spain had a tradition of good taste and writers of sound judgment to mitigate and finally to overcome the
malady; but Mexico had neither. As a result
the decadence in the colony was more nearly
complete than in Spain and persisted long after
the revival of art in the homeland. No other
influence produced such harmful results in the

---

[1]*Ibid.*, p. 106.
    [There comes over the salty sea from Spain
To our Mexican shores
A man crude and homeless
Weak in health and poor in worldly goods.
    And then as he acquires money and courage,
Others like him in their barbarous councils
Put on his head of Caesar and Virgil,
The two crowns of laurel and oak.
And so he who sold lace and pins
In the street is now a count,
In quality and in riches a Fúcar:
And he afterwards despises the place where
He gained respectability and fortune
And where he used to drag his fishing net in Sanlúcar.]

development of Mexican literature of colonial days as this substitution of verbal agility for profundity.

Poetry, history, religious writings and oratory were alike affected. The clergy, which had in the sixteenth century been absorbed in the serious task of establishing schools and evangelizing the natives, turned its energies into artificial rhetoric. Pompous vacuity replaced the deep mysticism of the school of Fray Luis de León. To understand the obscurity of forced metaphors and to use them in writing was more to be desired than to understand reality and present it in intelligible terms.

But in spite of the decadence of literature in the seventeenth century in Mexico, that literature had its values. The results of a century of vigorous activity on the part of educational institutions directed by men who were intent on raising the culture of Mexico to the level of that of the mother-country were becoming apparent in the enlightened society of the capital. Two of the products of that society are worthy of mention among the world's great writers. They have added to the world's permanent store of values.

Juan Ruiz de Alarcón, born in Mexico in 1581, went to Spain in 1600 to continue his education. He returned to his native land in 1608. Most of his works were written in Spain, where he lived from 1613 until his death; but he was largely the product of his native Mexico. While the work of this genius does not compare quantitatively with that of Lope de Vega or of Tirso de Molina, from a qualitative standpoint it was unsurpassed during the Golden Age of the Spanish drama. In penetration and logical development of character, in correctness of form, in integration of action and in harmony of plan Ruiz de Alarcón's work is unique. On the comedy of customs and ethics he left the stamp of his culture, a culture absorbed at least in part from Mexican society during his youth.

The other writer of the seventeenth century whose note of sincerity and genuine beauty was in strange contrast to the artificial eloquence of the times was Sor Juana Inés de la Cruz.

Born in 1651, Juana Inés de Asbaje very early acquired a passionate interest in the study of literature and of the various sciences taught in Mexico at that time. At the age of five she could read and write with remarkable ease and understanding. She is said to have mastered Latin in twenty lessons. So extensive was her knowledge that forty specialists selected by the Viceroy from different fields of learning were unable to confuse her. She was made one of the ladies-in-waiting in the viceregal palace.

But the soul of Juana aspired to greater heights than that of political favors, social prominence and ease. She renounced the world and entered a convent, taking the name Sor Juana Inés de la Cruz. She made of her cell a library, a laboratory and a studio of music. Her intellectual curiosity led her to study and investigate and to meditate on life and its concomitants. At times her poetic genius and inherent honesty of soul gave to her work a sincerity and genuineness that are in strange contrast with the artificiality characteristic of the period in which she lived. She was the only writer of her generation that was not consistently decadent.

During the last half of the eighteenth century there set in a neo-classical reaction against the decadence of the preceding epoch. This reaction was merely a delayed response to the spirit of reform in Spain, where the eighteenth century was devoted largely to removal of debris and to the laying of a critical foundation, with comparatively little original literary production.

At the beginning of the nineteenth century Mexican poets were building their art with the vestiges of Gongorism and the comparatively more recent pseudoclassicism that had been the most pronounced trend of Spanish poetry since the accession of the Bourbons at the beginning of the eighteenth century. The most respected guides were the preceptists of eighteenth-century Spain. But symptoms of change were not lacking.

Fray Manuel Martínez de Navarrete had displayed under his cloak of formal neo-classicism a sincerity and tenderness and rich imagination that had carried the seeds of change. Sartorio, the bulk of whose works are tainted with the aridity and prosaism of the eighteenth century, broke away in the latter part of his life, at least in practically all aspects except the purely formal one, and under the two powerful urges of mysticism and patriotism sang passionately to the Virgin and to his country. Anastasio María de Ochoa y Acuña, while relatively unimportant in Mexican poetry was one of a transitional group between the school of the eighteenth century and the romantic school. He added an important factor that González Peña called "a certain picturesque national spirit."[1] González Peña stated correctly that Ochoa was in poetry what Fernández de Lizardi was in prose, "the best painter of the social life of Mexico at the end of the colonial regime . . ."[2]

It was at this point that the noise of the revolution silenced all poetry except subversive fables and epigrams, hastily composed and without literary merit. But the violent heat of the period cast poetry into new molds, gave it a social mission. A sense of nationalism was born, and with it came a new heroic emphasis in poetry. The pamphleteers had been forced to use the language of the people and to deal with the background, physical and social, of Mexico. These new factors became a permanent part of Mexico's literary art.

But such developments were not independent of Spanish literature. Spain was passing through experiences similar to those of Mexico, and it

[1]*Ibid.*, p. 237.
[2]*Ibid.*, p. 237.

was quite natural that the colony should follow closely the literary models furnished by the homeland.

With the French invasion of 1808, poetry in Spain took a turn that was almost immediately followed in Mexico. José Manuel Quintana, already interested in the great personages of Spanish history, became a radiating source of patriotism illustrated in *A España, después de la revolución de marzo,* an ode sufficiently ardent to inspire one of Spain's most romantic poets to write *A la patria.* Álvarez de Cienfuegos y Acero, dissatisfied with the prosaic and artificial frigidity of neo-classicism, sounded a note of sentimentalism of romantic nature. Such works as *Mi paseo solitario en primavera, La escuela del sepulcro* and *La rosa del desierto* are among the first flickers of the dawn of romanticism, both in substance and in form. Juan Nicasio Gallego's most constant preoccupation was the love of Spain. His *El dos de mayo,* though showing the restraint of classicism more than some of Quintana's works, reveals an increasing tide of exalted patriotism that could not be contained entirely in a neo-classical frame. It was quite natural that the examples of poets like these were followed enthusiastically by Mexican poets.

It was this patriotic tendency of the mother country that gave inspiration and direction to the ardent patriots in Mexico. But that patriotism was not exclusively a characteristic of the romanticists. It was common to the works of both groups. The line of cleavage was evident only in the treatment accorded the patriotic motif.

In general the politically conservative class carried on the neo-classical tradition, while the liberal group, almost identical with the middle class, turned away from that tradition in search of new guides. The former were better educated and schooled in the disciplines of neo-classicism. The liberals, lacking in intellectual and artistic experience, veered rather sharply toward the destructive attitudes of Voltaire and the French encyclopedists in general and accepted eagerly the guidance of European romanticism in so far as their abilities and training permitted. Of them Urbina remarked:

Salieron desenfrenados, incorrectos, desbaratando reglas, rompiendo disciplinas, en un libertinaje retórico y prosódico que ponía espanto en el bando aristocrático de los clásicos a la española. El gemido esplenético, el sentimentalismo que se torna sensi-

blería, la vaguedad ideológica, la desesperacíon y
el hastío, la duda del bien, la obsesión de la muerte. . .[1]

But the emotion of patriotism was present in
both groups. It manifested itself in poetry, in
drama, and in prose.

The conservative group of post-revolution
poets, including Ortega, Castillo de Lanzas, Sánchez de Tagle, Manuel Carpio, J. J Pesado, Roa
Bárcena, together with Ignacio Ramírez, an arch-
liberal, Arango y Escandón and others, held to
their tradition of neo-classicism in general, but
instilled new life into it by the application of
the principles of the classicism of Spain's Gold-
en Age as well as that of Greece and Rome.
They could not, however, escape entirely the
influence of the virile spirit of romanticism that
pervaded so much of the literature of their day.
The one factor in the writings of this group that

---

[1]Luis G. Urbina: *La vida literaria de México,* Madrid, 1917, p. 151.

[They set to work without discipline, incorrect,
destroying rules, throwing off all restraint, in a
rhetorical and prosodic libertinism that frightened
the aristocratic group of classicists in the Spanish
manner. Splenetic groans, sentimentalism that becomes an abuse of sensitivity, ideological vagueness, desperation and boredom, doubt of goodness,
the obsession of death.]

is most important for our present purposes is
the spirit of nationalism and civic patriotism,
for it parallels the dominant preoccupation of
most of Mexico's historical novelists.

Of the early romantic poets and dramatists
we shall have more to say in the discussion of
the development of romanticism in Mexico to
which, because of its close connection with the
historical novel, is assigned a separate chapter.

C. THE DEVELOPMENT OF LIBERALISM AND ROMAN-
     TICISM IN MEXICAN THOUGHT AND ART AS DETER-
     MINING FACTORS IN THE HISTORICAL NOVEL

The world-wide trend toward liberalism that
characterized the beginning of the nineteenth
century, proceeding largely from the spirit of
the French Revolution, found a ready response
in Mexico as well as in other parts of Spanish
America. Hidalgo, the father of the revolution,
and Fernández de Lizardi, its chief pamphleteer, were inspired by the reading of liberal
writings, especially those of French origin, to
bring about the destruction of the old regime.
Added to the strength of this influence was the
wave of liberalism from Spain, of which the
Constitución de Cádiz of 1812 was a result. In
Mexico and in her sister colonies all classes ex-

cept the conservative group were predisposed toward enthusiastic acceptance of that liberalism because of their social and economic maladjustment. The emergence of a class consciousness among the Indians and mixed breeds and the resentment of the Creoles against the local Spanish ruling class had prepared the country for ideas of reform.

The long agitation for independence and the comparatively greater freedom of expression that existed after Iturbide's downfall stimulated the formation of a liberal group that, though almost entirely without discipline and tradition, became the champion of a vaguely conceived social and economic renovation. There was a quickening of interest in Mexico's past and in the development of liberal institutions in other countries. During the second half of the century the heroes of the movement toward independence became immensely popular in periodical literature and assumed the aspect of political saints. The institutions and leaders of the old regime were used in the roles of malicious opposition. The materials for historical fiction were abundant and the enthusiasm of a small group of young writers stirred them to use it.

Influences from abroad added their weight to the literary and intellectual reform. Among the *young intellectuals* there was lively curiosity concerning the thought trends and the history of other peoples. Translations of foreign works, with which Spain had been flooded, found their way into Mexico. Most prominent among these were the works of Voltaire, Rousseau, Goethe, Chateaubriand, Mme. de Stael, Benjamin Constant, Mme. Genlis, Mme. Cottin, Lamartine, Bernardin de Saint Pierre, d'Arlincourt, Scott and Byron.

These two interests, foreign thought and Mexico's past, were decisive of the trends of much of Mexican literature throughout the century. Some indication of prominence of these trends may be had from an examination of the contents of early Mexican magazines. In the *Semanario de las Señoritas,* (1841-1842), for instance, the following articles on foreign literature are found:

Vol. I.

Julieta, heroína de la tragedia de Shakespeare, p. 49.

Rebeca, heroína de la célebre novela de Walter Scott, p. 65.

Traducción de los versos de la esposa de Lord Byron, p. 105.

Pablo y Virginia, p. 137.

Flora MacIvor, heroína de Waverly (Walter Scott), p. 169.

Miranda, heroína de la Tempestad de Shakespeare, p. 305.

Pensamientos de Chateaubriand, p. 419.

Rosalinda, Deschamps, p. 457.

Celia (Shakespeare), p. 460.

Vol. II.

Evelina Berenger, heroína del Condestable de Chester de Walter Scott, p. 49.

Lucía Ashton, esposa de Lammermoor (Scott), p. 273.

Casandra, heroína de Troila y Cresida (Shakespeare), p. 289.

Jessica, heroína de El mercado de Venecia, p. 409.

Porcia, heroína de El mercado de Venecia, p. 412.

In the *Liceo mexicano,* 1844, the following articles deal with the history of the New World:

Vol. I.

Carlos M. Saavedra: *Malintzin o Da. Marina,* pp. 37-44.

R. I. Alcaraz: *Hernán Cortés,* pp. 91-109.

Various authors: *Galería de los virreyes de México.*

(This series of articles was continued in the second volume. In all there are twenty-two articles on the viceroys.)

D. Revilla: *Estudios históricos de independencia,* pp. 177-184.

Vol. II.

Carlos M. Saavedra: *Prisión y muerte del Inca Tupac Amaru,* pp. 10-13.

    Historia del Perú; controversias de jurisdicción, pp. 67-71.

    Manco Cápac o Yumpangi, pp. 194-198 and 218-222.

A. Rodríguez: *Primer viaje de Colón. Descubrimiento del Nuevo Mundo,* pp. 174-177.

Anon.: *La visión de Moctezuma,* pp. 345-350.

Anon.: *Tlahuicole, leyenda mexicana,* pp. 236-239.

El Museo Mexicano, 1844, was founded to record the deeds of great men of the past and the episodes incident to the development of Mexican nationalism. It contains numerous articles on historical personages, on antiquities and on the institutions of colonial times. There are in volumes two, three, and four, thirty-seven historical discourses by el Lic. D. José María Lacunza. The following list will give some idea of the nature of the material contained in the articles of historical nature, exclusive of the discourses of Lacunza mentioned above:

Manuel Payno: *Don Francisco Eduardo Tres-Guerras,* II, p. 16.

    El General Don Manuel de Mier y Terán, II, p. 121.

    Los primeros tiempos de la libertad mexicana, II, 182.

    Recuerdos de Don Pedro Escobedo, III, 62.

    Leyenda del año de 1648. *Trinidad de Juárez,* III, 289.

    Hechos históricos, IV, 119.

Mariano Otero: *Apuntes para la biografía de Francisco Javier Gamboa,* II, 53.

Manuel G. Pedraza: *Biografía mexicana. D. Miguel Ramos Arizpe,* II, 105.

D. Revilla: *Estudios históricos. Arroyo hondo*, II, 138.
Guillermo Prieto: *Escenas de la vida del General Don José María Morelos y Pavón*, Vol. II, p. 163.
D. Revilla: *27 de septiembre de 1821*, II, 231.
El Marqués del Valle: *Documentos relativos a Hernán Cortés*, II, p. 275.
Redacción: *Antigüedades zapotecas*, III, 135.
        Simón Bolívar, III, 310.

An announcement on page 397 of the *Revista Mexicana*, Mexico, 1835, gives a little light on the foreign works available in translation in the book stores of Mexico. The list includes:

Bursk: *Reflecsiones sobre la revolución de Francia.*
Walter Scott: *Waverly o ahora sesenta años.*
        El Abad.
Lourdoueiz: *Las locuras del día.*
Cottin: *La Malvina.*
Samuel Johnson: *Historia de Rasselas.*
Piccard: *El Gil Blas de la revolución.*
Arlincourt: *El solitario.*
        La extranjera, o la muger misteriosa.
Ana Radcliffe: *Julia.*
Swift: *Viages del Capitán Gulliver.*
Mme. Genlis: *El sitio de la Rochela.*

For several reasons the romantic trend in literature appealed to Mexican writers. In the first place it represented in general the same basic spirit of rebellion and renovation in letters that had been the motivation of the liberals in political and social fields. In the second place, the intimate sentimentalism, the emotive procedure, the lyricism of ideas and the sublimation of life's deeper experiences, all characteristic of romanticism, were in consonance with basic Mexican racial characteristics. G. Urbina correctly summarized this predisposition thus:

> ... poseíamos los elementos psíquicos; la expresión nos vino de fuera; la emoción la teníamos ya; era nuestra desde hacía muchos años.[1]

In this same connection he called attention to

> El medio de agitación y de conmoción incesantes; nuestras costumbres caballerescas y legendarias; ... la vida popular de hampa y truhanería; la profunda división en las ideas, que engendraba delirantes afectos y frenéticos odios; la inquietud espiritual; la ancestral inclinación al sentimentalismo y al ensueño; los contrastes y antítesis de una existencia en la que iban revueltos místicos que leían a Santa Teresa y ateos que estudiaban a los enciclopedistas; ...[2]

---

[1]*Ibid.*, p. 143.

[... we possessed the psychic elements; the expression came to us from without; we already had the emotion ; it had been ours for many years.]

[2]*Ibid.*, pp. 142-143.

[The atmosphere of incessant agitation and commotion; our chivalrous and legendary customs; ... the popular life of knavery and vagabondage; the profound division in ideas, which engendered unreasoning affection and mad hatreds; the spiritual inquietude; the ancestral inclination toward sentimentalism and dreaming; the contrasts and antitheses of an existence in which mystics who read Santa

In the third place, independent Mexico, lacking the maturity necessary for originality, naturally fell in line with the movement dominant in Europe, especially in Spain. Furthermore, romanticism gave opportunity to writers who were without the discipline, formal and logical, necessary for literary work of classical or even of neo-classical emphasis.

But the most important predisposing factors were the racial characteristics and the almost universal dispersion of the ferment of romanticism as the basic philosophy of human thought. In order to fix more definitely the more immediate origins and characteristics of this movement in Mexico, some of which were distinctly Mexican, it will be necessary to examine the works of the first two romantic poets and dramatists of Mexican literature. These two writers were Fernando Calderón and Ignacio Rodríguez Galván.

In 1828 Fernando Calderón, then nineteen years of age, published in Guadalajara a volume of the poetry he had written up to that date. In these poems of his childhood there is discern-

Teresa and atheists who studied the encyclopedists opposed each other.]

ible for the first time in the works of a Mexican
writer of recognized merit a definite shift to
romantic attitudes. His later works, including
dramatic compositions, became increasingly romantic.

In Calderón's work there are several characteristics that became outstanding in Mexican romanticism; a profound and lyric melancholy
emanating from the Amerind racial spirit, man-
ifesting itself in the idea of death as a poetic
preoccupation, in the rapture and the despair of
love, and in a sense of frustration in ideals; an
exalted chivalry that admits of no middle ground
between nobility of soul and depravity. A few
examples will suffice to illustrate.

In *El porvenir*, written in 1825 when the author was sixteen years old, Calderón, inspired
with the lyric idea of death and final separation
from his lover, sings:

> Tú me amas y yo te adoro;
> Pero ha de llegar el día
> en que tú o yo para siempre
> debemos dejar la vida:
> .   .   .   .
>
> No temas, Amira hermosa,
> De horrible muerte las iras;
> Las almas que el cielo junta
> ¿Quién pudiera desunirlas?

> No; nuestro amor será eterno:
> A otra más brillante vida
> Renacerán a adorarse
> Tus cenizas y las mías.[1]

In *De mi amor a Delia,* as in most of his other love poems, he sang his passionate love and the limitless joys and boundless sorrow it brought him.

> En momentos tan felices
> Mi alma ardiente se elevaba,
> Y horas enteras pasaba
> Embriagado en mi placer;
> Pero se corría este velo
> Y viéndome desgraciado,
> Volvía a mi funesto estado
> De llorar y padecer.[2]

---

[1]Fernando Calderón: *Obras poéticas,* México, segunda edición, 1850, pp. 1-2.

> [You love me and I love you
> But there must come a day
> In which either you or I
> Must leave this life forever:
>
> .   .   .   .
>
> Do not fear, beautiful Amira,
> The wrath of horrible death;
> For souls that heaven unites,
> Who could put them asunder?
> No; our love will be eternal:
> Into another brighter life
> Your ashes and mine
> Will be born to love again.]

[2]*Ibid.,* p. 399.

> [In moments of such bliss

There are love of nature and a sense of kinship with it in *El amor en la campaña*. Typical
are the lines

> Sí; allí bajo los árboles sombríos
> Contento viviré, sin fin vagando,
> Ya mirando correr los anchos ríos,
> O con humilde cítara cantando,
> En presencia del campo de las flores
> El desdichado fin de mis amores.
>
> Tal vez el hondo valle
> Resonará con mi doliente queja,
>   Y la inocente oveja
> Dejará de pacer por escucharla,
> O bien subiendo a la elevada cima
>   Del monte majestuoso
>   Invocaré el reposo,
> Y el alivio del fuego que me anima:
> Sí, yo no dudo que me escuche el cielo
> Y me mande piadoso algún consuelo.[1]

> My raptured soul was wafted high,
> And entire hours I passed
> Drunk on joy.
>
> But this mask was taken off
> And thinking on my hapless lot,
> I was again earth's child begot
> For weeping and for sorrow.]

[1]*Ibid.*, p. 406.

> [Yes; there under the somber trees
> I shall live content a wanderer,
> Watching the broad river flow,
> Or with an humble cithern singing
> Among the meadows and the flowers
> The sad end of my love.

In *Mi tristeza* the writer returns to the poetry of grief.

> Ecsala (sic) pesarosa el alma mía
> Suspiros tiernos en la noche oscura;
> De dolor lleno, lleno de amargura
> Me encuentra sin cesar el claro día.
>   Tristeza es solamente mi elemento
> Tristeza en derredor tan solo miro;
> Tristeza engendra en mí también el viento
> Que siempre lo trasformo en un suspiro.[1]

Much of Calderón's poetry of this type was the result of the deep impression he received from the works of Lamartine, some of which he

---

Perhaps the deep valley
Will echo my doleful complaint,
And the innocent ewe
Will stop her grazing to listen.
Or climbing to the lofty peaks
of majestic mountains
I shall invoke repose
And relief from the fires that within me burn.
I doubt not that heaven will hear me
And being moved, will send me peace.]

[1]*Ibid.*, p. 409.

[My heavy heart gives forth
Tender sighs in the dark night;
Full of grief and bitterness
The daylight always finds me.
  Sadness is my element,
Sadness in all around I see:
And the wind arouses sadness in me,
For I always transform it into sighs.]

translated into Spanish. In some of his poems he
imitated Espronceda. His *El soldado de la
libertad* is in form and movement almost identical with Espronceda's *Canción del pirata.*
But there is a significant difference between
the two. Instead of saying with Espronceda's
pirate "my law (is) force and the wind, my
only fatherland the sea", Calderón's soldier
sang "I seek in war liberty or death". The latter was fighting for the freedom of his country;
the former was a picturesque rebel against society and its moral traditions. Such rebellion
against traditional morality is foreign to Mexican romanticism, for with all the emphasis Mexican romanticists put on the destruction of the
institutions of the colonial regime, there is no
attack on traditional ideas of morality. There
is rather severe condemnation of the old regime
for its failure to put into practice moral principles then accepted in all Christian lands.

In his romantic dramas Calderón is European even in his choice of material. He sought
European subjects with a medieval setting. *El
torneo* (1839) is a historical drama set in England in the eleventh century. It is the story of
two lovers separated by the will of the girl's

father. Isabel was to be married against her
will to a baron of renown. Just before the wedding a strange woman interrupted the feast with
an equally strange story. She revealed the fact
that she was the wife of the baron's brother,
whom the former had killed. The baron had
then disposed of the woman's son and had put
her in a dungeon in order to inherit the family
estate. But the woman had escaped from her
prison and had come to accuse the murderer
and usurper. A boyish knight, the lover of Isabel, avenged the woman by killing the baron in
a duel. An accomplice of the dead baron then
revealed that this young knight was the lost son
of the baron's brother and of the strange woman,
and that since he was of noble blood, he was
worthy of the hand of Isabel.

Ana Bolena (1842) has its setting in England
in 1536. Like *El torneo*, it follows the trend of
European romantic dramas with a medieval
setting, and it contains little that is distinctively
Mexican. The same is true of *Herman, o la vuelta
del cruzado* (1842), which has its setting in
Germany in the twelfth century.

The second romantic poet and dramatist of
Mexican letters was Ignacio Rodríguez Galván

(1816-1842).   Of native stock, he passed his
early life in the poverty to which his race was
heir. In 1827 he went to work in his maternal
uncle's bookstore.   In his leisure moments he
read avidly.   Having taught himself to read
French, he formed his literary tastes by reading the romantic works of French and Spanish
authors. With his poetry and dramas romanticism became firmly established in Mexico.

Launching himself into a literary career with
only his racial instinct as a guide, he wrote without formality, but in keeping with the spirit of
his people. To the notes sounded by Calderón
he added others: the poetic theme of oppression, of tyranny and injustice; exalted acts of
self-sacrifice under the powerful urges of patriotism and loyalty to ideals; the conflict of
love with duty to country; and virtue that maintains itself unspotted in the face of death. Like
the vows of ancient knights, Rodríguez Galván's
creed requires the protection of virtue and the
glorification of justice.   In his *El buitre*
(1837), he tells what he would do if he were
an enormous vulture. One by one he mentions
the classes of unjust humans that his beak would
destroy. The tyrant, the seducer, the robber of

widows and children, the traitor, all these would
shed their blood until the earth should become
a sea of blood. Then the vulture would find repose. Each stanza ends with the refrain, "If I
had been born a frightful vulture, my vengeance would make me immortal".

This attitude was held firmly by most of Mexico's romanticists, sometimes expressed crudely,
sometimes in truly artistic form, sometimes with
great sincerity, sometimes in parrot-like fashion, but always with vehemence. Mexican romanticism was severely righteous. There is no
other feature that stands out so prominently as
this. Justice and right, nobility and loyalty became a religion to the early romanticists of the
youthful Mexican nation.

In Rodríguez Galván's drama is to be found
another application of romanticism to Mexican
idealology. Much of Europe's romanticism was
traditional; nearly all of Mexico's was liberal.
European romanticists found much interest and
beauty inherent in their middle ages. Mexican
romanticists found an equally great interest in
the conquest period and in colonial times. Inter-
preting those periods in terms of their nineteenth-century liberalism, they found them full

of monstrous iniquities. There was oppression, there was tyranny, there was injustice that kindled the flames of idealistic justice into roaring conflagrations. The conquest and colonial times were replete with forces that served to frustrate liberal aspirations. This poetic interpretation of Mexico's past in terms of the conventions of nineteenth century ideology is quite distinct from the artistic *resurrection* that many Europeans attempted in dealing with the middle ages of Europe. Scott, for instance, tried to escape from his century and return to the spirit of the past; Mexican historical novelists who dealt with the distant past attempted to interpret that past in terms of their own nineteenth-century thought.

This tendency, so evident in the first class of Mexican historical novels to which attention was called in the preface, namely, the novels that deal with the conquest and with colonial times, is present in some of Rodríguez Galván's historical dramas and in several of his poems. In *Profecía de Guatimoc* (1839) the poet identifies independent Mexico with the Amerind regime, considering the former a restoration of the latter after an interruption of three centuries that resulted from the temporary conquest achieved by invaders from Europe. The ghost of Guatimocín, ancient king of Anáhuac, is made to weep over the cruelties of the invaders to his people. With great pathos he exclaims:

> Nada perdona el bárbaro europeo
> Todo lo rompe, y tala, y aniquila
> Con brazo furibundo.[1]
>
> Es su placer en fúnebres desiertos
> Las ciudades trocar (¡Hazaña honrosa!)
> Ve el sueño con desdén, si no reposa
> Sobre insepultos muertos.[2]
>
> ¿Lloras, pueblo infeliz y miserable?
> ¿A qué sirve tu llanto?
> ¿Qué vale tu lamento?
> Es tu agudo quebranto
> Para el hijo de Europa inaplacable
> Su más grato alimento.[3]

---

[1] Ignacio Rodriguez Galván: *Obras*, México, 1876, Vol. I, p. 268.

[The barbarous European pardons nothing;
He breaks, he devastates, he annihilates
With furious arm.]

[2] *Ibid.*, Vol. I, p. 268.

[His delight is to turn into desert wastes
All inhabited places (Honorable exploits, indeed!)
His sleep is not serene if on dead bodies
He does not pillow his head.]

[3] *Ibid.*, Vol. I, p. 269.

[Do you weep, unhappy people and miserable?
And what do your tears bring you?
Of what avail is your lamentation?

Then the author sounds a warning that is a prophecy of Mexican freedom:

> El que del infeliz el llanto vierte,
> Amargo llanto verterá angustiado;
> El que huella al endeble, será hollado,
> El que la muerte da, recibe muerte.[1]

Tyranny was severely condemned in Moctezuma because it was a violation of Amerind ideals. In *La visión de Moctezuma* (1842) an old Indian woman who had been beaten by tax-gatherers of the emperor drowned in the lake while attempting to swim after the boat in which the emperor, Moctezuma himself, was carrying off her daughter. Later her ghost appeared to Moctezuma and foretold the coming of the Spaniards. She then disappeared, leaving the emperor downcast. A messenger soon brought news of the arrival of strange men off the coast. They were the *conquistadores*.

Your deep despair
Is for the implacable European
His sweetest food.]
[1]*Ibid.*, Vol. I, p. 271.

[He who draws the tears of grief from unhappy eyes
Will weep the bitter tears of anguish;
He who tramples on the helpless shall be trampled.
He who kills wantonly shall reap the harvest of death.]

With *Muñoz, Visitador de México* (1838), Rodríguez Galván established the romantic drama based on Mexico's early history. The theme is the arrogant tyranny of Muñoz in Mexico in the year 1567. This infamous representative of the Spanish king set his eyes on Celestina, virtuous wife of Sotelo, and determined to break her will by threatening to kill her husband and her adopted child if she refused to consort with him. But virtue did not fall, even after the tyrant had carried out his threat. Celestina died of grief and exhaustion, embracing the dead body of her husband. So strong was the writer's conviction of the utter depravity of Muñoz that he had him exclaim as he looked on his victims, "Even I detest myself."

In this drama is to be seen another instance of the tendency of Mexican romanticists to project their nineteenth-century ideals into the past. The facts of colonial history are interpreted in the light of nineteenth-century ideals of chivalry, of freedom, of justice and of moral right. Again attention may be called to the fact that this same procedure was adopted almost universally by writers of Mexican historical novels based on the conquest and on colonial times.

El privado del virrey, finished in 1841 and published in 1842, has a similar theme, authority used to force the will of a virtuous woman. In this case the distracted woman is forced to submit as the price of her husband's life. The setting is in Mexico in 1640 and 1641.

In both these dramas there is the usual violent hatred of the tyranny and licentiousness of European invaders. It is significant that the tyranny of Moctezuma as revealed in *La visión de Moctezuma* was an evil alien to the Amerind spirit, while that of the Europeans was considered to be inherent in European civilization. Under the heel of the Spaniards Garcerán Tezozomoc, a descendant of the ancient Aztec royal line, was made to remark:

> ¡He visto tanta venganza
> Tanto asesinato frío
> Y auto de fe, y desafío
> Y tanta y tanta matanza!
> Y es tal mi miseria impía
> Que, por divertir mi suerte,
> Abrazado con la muerte,
> Tranquilo me dormiría.[1]

---

[1]*Ibid.*, Vol. II, p. 215.

> [So much vengeance I have seen,
> So much cruel assassination,
> So much inquisition and arrogance,
> So much slaughter and carnage,

In *Muñoz, Visitador de México*, the author gives eloquent expression to his noble aspiration for freedom. Pedro de Quesada, discussing the determination of his group to rid Mexico of tyrants, declaims:

> Si vamos a perecer
> Grabaremos nuestros nombres
> En la historia de los hombres
> Que libres supieron ser.[1]

D. THE MORE IMMEDIATE ORIGINS OF THE MEXICAN NOVEL

Early Stories and the Works of Fernández de Lizardi

One cannot escape being impressed by the almost total absence of worthwhile fiction in Mexico during the colonial regime, especially in view of the popularity of the genre in Spain up to the eighteenth century. Critics have supposed that the severe laws prohibiting the ship-

---

> And so hopeless is my misery
> That to change my sad estate
> I could go to sleep serene
> In the arm of kindly death.]

[1]*Ibid.*, Vol. II, p. 87.
> [And if we perish
> Let us engrave our names
> In the history of men
> Who have known how to be free.]

ment of novels into the colonies left the latter
without contact with that type of literaure. Such
conclusions are untenable in the light of recent
studies made by Irving A. Leonard. An examination of fragmentary official lists of books
shipped to the colonies reveals the fact that the
prohibition of the importation of fiction was frequently disregarded.[1]

Of all books shipped, from seventy-five to
eighty-five per cent were theological or doctri-
nal. The class of secular works brought in indicates that in poetry, in drama and in the novel
colonial tastes followed faithfully though tard-
ily the trends in Spain. The vogue of *Amadís de
Gaula* and its successors, of *Diana* and of *Laza-
rillo de Tormes* in the homeland was transferred
to the colonies. The registers show that the novels
of chivalry were the most popular type of fiction
during the sixteenth century and that they began
to lose ground after 1590, being replaced largely
by pastoral novels. But these two types continued for some time, represented mainly by
highly sentimental imitations of earlier stories.

---

[1]Irving A. Leonard: *Romances of Chivalry in the
Spanish Indies . . ,* in *University of California Publications in Modern Philology,* Vol. XVI, No. 3, p. 219 *et seq.*

The largest single shipment of books of chivalry on record, according to Leonard, was made in 1601, but there were very few of this type of shipments made after that date. At the beginning of the seventeenth century the picaresque novel became popular. It is clear from the size of the shipments that the colonists were more interested in reading than has been supposed. One list shows a total of ten thousand books sent by one dealer at one time, and lists of one thousand are not uncommon.[1] The lack of production of fiction in New Spain then is not chargeable to lack of contacts with the novels of Spain.

But it is a fact that in spite of New Spain's acquaintance with Spanish fiction, over ten thousand publications are mentioned in bibliographies of the presses of Mexico before the publication of *El Periquillo*, (1816), the first true novel published in New Spain. The novel did not flourish anywhere in Spanish America during the colonial period. It will be remembered also that the English colonies produced no novel until after they gained their independence. This phenomenon cannot be charged to censorship, for the novel has never flourished

[1]*Ibid.*

in immature societies, censored or uncensored. There was not enough social, intellectual and spiritual heritage in New Spain to produce fiction.

There had been, however, attempts at narrative prose prior to the nineteenth century. The first was Francisco Bramón's *Los sirgueros de la Virgen sin original pecado*, (1620). It is mentioned in Medina's *La Imprenta en México* with the following comments:

> Es una fábula pastoril, parecida a la *Galatea* de Cervantes. Y por ser poco usada la palabra *sirgueros* quiero decir que significa cantos, de la voz griega *sir;* y ésta es la etimología de la voz vulgar castellana *Gilguero o Xilguero* ... Don Francisco be Bramón, natural de la N. E., bachiller y consiliario de la Universidad de México. Fué sin duda uno de los buenos poetas de la América.[1]

Medina adds the comment that there are many poems scattered through the body of the work.

---

[1]Medina: *La imprenta en México*, Santiago de Chile, 1909, Vol. II, p. 87.

[It is a pastoral tale, similar to the *Galatea* of Cervantes. And because the word *sirgueros* is little used I wish to explain that it means *songs,* from the Greek root *sir;* and this is the etymology of the current Spanish word *gilguero* or *xilguero* ... Don Francisco de Bramón, a native of New Spain, bachelor of arts and member of the council of the University of Mexico. He was without doubt one of the good poets of America.]

It has been impossible to procure a copy of this work for examination. The few references available lead to the conclusion that the work is a primitive pastoral story.

The second prose work of narrative nature published in Mexico was *Sucesos de Fernando o la caída de Fernando*, by Antonio Ochoa, of which only its name is now known.

The third work of this type in Mexican colonial literature was *Los Infortunios de Alonso Ramírez*, an artless summary of episodes that might have been used as a plot for a novel. But nothing more than plot exists in it, and even that is crude. It is the story of a boy who ran away from home to better his fortune. Sailing as cabin boy to Captain Juan del Corcho, he touched at Havana and thence went to San Juan de Ulúa. After a hard journey to Puebla de Los Angeles, he served as apprentice to a carpenter for six months in order to escape starvation. He did not, however, escape privation. From Puebla he went to Mexico City and from there to Oaxaca to ask aid of a relative. Unsuccessful in this attempt to establish himself, he hired himself to a traveling merchant who took him to Chiapas and Guatemala. After the death of his employer he returned to Mexico City, and married a girl who later died of childbirth.

In desperate need, the young man sailed for the Philippine Island. He was captured by English pirates and carried half-way around the world. After suffering many abuses at the hands of the pirates he was released in a small ship without knowing where he was and without the instruments necessary for navigation. The author brought him through these harrowing experiences and finally landed him in Yucatán, from which place he went to Mexico City.

There is nothing in the story to appeal to the imagination of the reader, nothing to reveal to him the character of the boy, little of human reactions, nothing, in fact, of true fiction. It is the story of a dead man of long ago whom the author was unable to resurrect. The veil of generality does not permit a single intimate glimpse of him.

The *Peregrino con guía y medicina universal de la alma* (1750) of Reynel y Hernández, a teacher of theology in the *Seminario Tridentino de México,* is a complicated hotchpotch of mystic, didactic and narrative elements, with no evidence of plan or definite purpose.

González de Sancha wrote a work called *Fabiano y Aurelia* (1760) that closely approaches fiction; but it cannot properly be called a novel. Pimentel characterized it as a story of lascivious and indecent love affairs.[1]

None of these early narratives have anything to do with the development of the novel in Mexico. They had neither intrinsic value nor issue. For purposes of literary criticism Fernández de Lizardi must be considered the first Mexican novelist, and his *Periquillo Sarniento*, 1816, the first Mexican novel.

El Periquillo Sarniento follows rather closely the technique and procedure of the better known Spanish picaresque novels and adds thereto an almost constant moralizing didacticism. Written in a journalistic tone, without formal refinements of any kind, and full of annoying digressions that destroy its unity, the work nevertheless has substantial merits, especially for the student of origins in Mexican literature. It is the product of the aroused spirit of revolt and ferments of change that characterized the epoch in which it appeared. Its author has rightly been called the pamphleteer of the

---

[1] González Peña: *op. cit.,* p. 262.

revolution, and in this novel and others he is still to some extent a campaigning pamphleteer. Not until the time of Manuel Payno did Mexico produce another author who painted so realistically the life of the Mexican people. *El Periquillo* is more than a picture, however; it is a protest of a new sense of national identity against the regime that held sway in the revolutionary period. It is also an attack on social vices that had their roots in the moral decadence of the times.

La Quijotita y su prima (1818), essentially picaresque, shows the influence of Rousseau's *Emile* in its preoccupation with the education of women as a determining factor in their character. Its primary interest for us in this connection is its spirit of social criticism that was a part of the movement toward liberalism and reform.

Vida y hechos del famoso caballero D. Catrín de la Fachenda brings under severe scrutiny the parasitic dandy of the colonial regime. It is not essentially different from *El Periquillo* except in the matter of the class to which the protagonist belonged.

In the partially autobiographical *Noches tristes y día alegre* (1818) there is visible a rather marked influence emanating from the pre-romantic *Noches lúgubres* (about 1771) of Cadalso, who in turn had found inspiration in the *Night Thoughts* of Edward Young. González Peña said of this work:

> . . . es la primera manifestación de la influencia del pre-romanticismo europeo en las letras mexicanas.[1]

The vogue of Lizardi in literary circles was surprisingly great. Until well beyond the middle of the nineteenth century he was the most popular Mexican author. Whether that was because he had no competition at first does not alter the fact that his popularity encouraged imitation even in his more unfortunate trends. Much of the weakness of Mexican fiction can be traced to the example set by Lizardi in the first stages of the novel's development in Mexico.

But the critic will recognize the fact that many of his weaknesses were quite natural in the period of transition in which Lizardi lived. He must be considered a projection of the eighteenth century with a superimposed spirit of renova-

---

[1] *Ibid.*, p. 268.
. . . it is the first manifestation of the influence of European pre-romanticism in Mexican letters.

tion and change. His works are a curious combination of the two. From the old he took his procedure; from the contemporary, his spirit. And precisely that is one of the major characteristics of early Mexican fiction.

The Short Historical Stories of the Early Nineteenth Century

During the third and fourth decades of the century there were many attempts to write short stories containing a fabrication of legend and popular historical material. Some of the most popular of these were: Gómez de la Cortina's *La calle de Don Juan Manuel,* published in *Revista Mexicana,* 1835, pp. 551-560; José Joaquín Pesado's *El inquisidor de México,* 1835; *El criollo,* by J. R. Pacheco, 1836; Rodríguez Galván's *La hija del oidor,* published in *El Año Nuevo,* 1837; *Pedro el bueno y Pedro el malo,* published in *El Álbum Mexicano,* 1849, and two short stories bearing the titles *Don Juan de Escobar* and *El visitador.* A short discussion of a few of these tales will not be amiss.

El inquisidor de México, a story of forty-three pages in the *Biblioteca de Autores Mexicanos* edition, deals with the Inquisition during colonial times. It, together with other shorter and less formal stories, is the forerunner of the series of novels on the same subject, beginning with *La hija del judío* of Justo Sierra and including several of the novels of Riva Palacio.

In his description of the inquisitorial procedure Pesado made his characters more real and human by refusing to impute to them the criminal hypocrisy and bad faith that was later the burden of Riva Palacio's monotonous stories; but he showed them to be rather the sincere and zealous victims of the delusions of their age. Whether that is accurate as history does not matter. It frees the author from the villain-hero complex that gives an amateurish note to much of Mexican fiction. Pesado penetrated deeper into human ills than those who sought their source only in human ill-will and villainy.

The author used as his main device an official's condemnation of a victim who turned out to be his close relative. The Inquisitor, don Domingo Ruiz de Guevara, condemned Sara and her lover along with other offenders. When all but Sara were burned and she was unconscious from the heat of the flames, the Inquisitor learned that she was his own daughter whom he had not seen since her childhood. Her rescue from the flames, her subsequent conversion, and her father's renunciation of his office reveal a very human weakness in both characters. This very weakness, however, seems natural.

Heavily charged with a consciousness of the social injustice that conflicted with the ideals of its day, *El criollo* by J. R. Pacheco is one of the best of the early historical tales, both from the standpoint of intrinsic interest and of literary interpretation of the spirit of the epoch.

It has an interesting basis in the caste system of colonial times, a system that made the most illustrious creole inferior to the most worthless individual born in the motherland. Because the creoles were considered unfit for marriage with Spaniards, a love affair between a Spanish girl and a creole son of highly respected Spanish parents came to a tragic end.

In the course of the story the author recreates the atmosphere of colonial life. A typical lady of high standing, for example, had received no education whatever, had never held an open book in her hands except in the act of reading brokenly from her prayer book. A sense of New Spain's intellectual isolation in colonial times pervades much of the book; indeed there it was generally believed that only Spain existed outside Mexico. This partially fantastic background serves admirably the author's purposes.

The hero of *El criollo* is made to seek death in the revolution started by Hidalgo, but nothing of importance concerning the revolution is included in the work.

La hija del oidor, by Ignacio Rodríguez Galván, dated November 27, 1836, is a pale story of twenty-three pages about the daughter of an *oidor* of the time when Archbishop Lizana was viceroy of Mexico. It is without logical progression and motivation, has no beauty of form or material and contains no portrayal of character. The author's deficiencies were the results of a misconception of the nature of romanticism as a literary movement. In romanticism he missed entirely the spiritual values and initiated the noisy and violent superficialities.

Netzula, by José María Lafragua, dated December 27, 1832, belongs to the cycle of stories concerning the Amerinds. Netzula, betrothed by her parents to Oxfeler without ever having seen him, fell in love with a stranger; but she sent the latter away because she thought their

union was impossible. Coming later to a battle-
field strewn with the victims of the Spaniards'
guns, she found the stranger she loved expiring. He was Oxfeler.

Angela, by Mariano Navarro, is the story of
an army officer who, in the revolution of 1810,
kidnapped, ravished and killed a girl who
proved to be his own daughter. It is without
interest.

Don Juan de Escobar and *El visitador*, both
anonymous, are short historical stories, the former dealing with the revolutionary period and
the latter with events of the year 1567. Their
only importance is in their role as manifesta-
tions of early interest in historical fiction.

Spanish Historical Novelists Who Wrote on Mexican Subjects Before 1850

The historical novelists of Mexico of the first
half of the nineteenth century found encouragement in the fact that some contemporary Spanish novelists were using events and characters of
the conquest and of colonial times in Mexico
as material for their romantic novels.

In 1838 Ignacio Manuel Pusalgas y Guerris

published in Barcelona his *El nigromántico
mejicano*. It is the story of the conquest of Mexico. In 1846 Gertrudis Gómez de Avellaneda
published *Guatimozín* in Madrid.   This work
was reprinted in Mexico in 1853 and again in
1857. There is an English translation by Blake,
published in Mexico in 1898. Patricio de la
Escosura, in 1850, published in Madrid and in
Mexico the first edition of his *La conjuración
de México o los hijos de Hernán Cortés*. It deals
with the conspiracy of the Marqués del Valle,
Cortés' son, and the Avila brothers to make the
Marqués ruler of Mexico.[1]

Of these novels the best known is *Guatimozín*
of Gertrudis Gómez de Avellaneda.   It is the
story of the fall of the Aztec empire rather
than a story of Cortés' triumph, for the main
interest throughout the book is centered around
the Amerinds. When he first appears in the
story, Motezuma is a very attractive and admirable figure, worthy of honor and respect, of extraordinary valor and ability, liberal, just, and
a warrior on whose face none of his many ene-

---

[1]Prof. William Zellers of Lakeland, Florida, whose
book on the historical novel of Spain will soon be off
the press, has kindly furnished from his bibliographical
files the two items of Pusalgas and Escosura.

mies in battle has ever seen a look of fear. But this same strong emperor becomes the victim of despair in the face of the dire prophecies of his superstitious priests. The reader finds himself deploring the superstitions that gradually loosen the cement of his character and make of him an impotent leader of his mighty people.

Cortés, on the other hand, is unscrupulous. He weighs with mathematical precision all courses of action and all forces, without moral consideration of any kind. He is like a shrewd demon with no compunctions of conscience. His own advantage is his only guide. People whose religious faith is different from his own are not considered humans by him. He is a thoroughly unattractive product of the religious fanaticism and inquisitorial spirit of his age.

Two of the most interesting features of the work are the poetic traditions of the Aztecs, based on a sense of fate that no mortal could resist or alter, and the idyllic love of Guatimozín for his beautiful wife and child. Guatimozín, the successor of Motezuma, is a perfect example of the epic hero of Spanish idealism. He is the Cid Campeador in a different setting, contending with odds which no man could overcome.

But Guatimozín's heroic spirit could not be defeated even in death. There is powerful tragedy in the episode involving the burning of this great chieftain in the presence of his wife. The strain was too great for the tender lady, accustomed only to the kind treatment her husband gave her, and her mind snapped under the burden of grief. But not one word of complaint did the tortured husband utter. Turning to a companion who was weeping with pain, he rebuked him and then asked, "And do you think I am on a bed of roses?"

The treatment these Spanish authors gave the episodes of the conquest and colonial times is essentially the same as that given the same events by Mexican authors. In fact, no Mexican author succeeded in making more noble and poetic the soul of his Amerind ancestors than did Gertrudis Gómez de Avellaneda in her *Guatimozín*. Her example gave encouragement and inspiration to later Mexican historical novelists of romantic inclinations.

CHAPTER II

FROM INDEPENDENCE TO THE REFORM
PERIOD

FIRST NOVELS

From 1800 to 1850 there were published not more than thirteen Mexican compositions that can be included in a very loose classification of the novel.[1] Of these only four have sufficient historical basis to justify mention as historical novels. These four will be discussed in chronological order.

Jicoténcal

The first of the latter group that can be even tentatively included in this study is *Jicoténcal*, published in 1826 in Philadelphia. The book contains no indication, either by direct state-

---

[1]These were:

Fernández de Lizardi: *El Periquillo Sarniento*, with three editions before 1850, bearing respectively the dates 1816, 1830, and 1842.

—— *Las noches tristes*, with four editions before 1850, dated 1818-1819, 1831, 1836 and 1843 respectively.

—— *La Quijotita y su prima*, with four editions before 1850, dated 1819, 1831, 1836 and 1842 respectively.

—— *Don Catrín de la Fachenda*, 1832.

Montes de Oca: *A través de la melancolía, cuentos*, 1822.

ment or internal evidence, as to the identity of the author. It is listed in the catalogue of the British Museum as a Spanish novel, but probably only because it is written in Spanish. The back side of the title page in both volumes contains this statement:

> ... Frederick Hutner hath deposited in this office the title of a book the right whereof he claims as proprietor in the words following, to wit: Jicoténcal ...

The insert immediately preceding the title page in both volumes has this statement:

> Se encontrará en Filadeltia en casa del Señor F. Merino, profesor de lengua castellana en el Instituto de Franklin; y en la del Señor J. Laval.[1]

Anon.: *Jicoténcal,* Philadelphia, 1826. (The author of this work, as stated in the text, has not been identified.)

Mariano Meléndez y Muñoz: *El misterioso,* 1836.

I. D. Castillo: *La prostitución o consecuencias de un mal ejemplo,* 1836.

Anon.: *El incógnito de la cabaña,* 1838.

Justo Sierra (Padre): *Un año en el Hospital de San Lázaro,* 1841.

—— *La hija del judío,* published in serial form, 1848-1850.

Manuel Payno: *El fistol del diablo,* 1845-1846.

Florencio del Castillo: *Horas de tristeza,* 1849.

[1]It will be found on sale in Philadelphia in the home of Mr. F. Merino, Professor of Spanish in Franklin Institute, and in that of Mr. J. Laval.

The *Manual del librero hispanoamericano* of Antonio Palau y Dulcet classifies the work as a Mexican historical novel, but probably only because it deals with Mexican history. It is not mentioned by Juan Iguíniz in his *Bibliografía de novelistas mexicanos*, but is listed in Arturo Rioseco's *Bibliografía de la novela mejicana*. Torres-Rioseco found it listed in the García Collection of the library of the University of Texas. Until the author's identity is established its inclusion here must be tentative.

The story is an unadorned informal chronicle made up of facts mixed with romantic fiction. It begins with a discussion of the fate awaiting the Republic of Tlascala at the hands of Cortés, who was then marching toward the capital city. By a clever ruse Cortés captured Teutila, the lover of Jicoténcal, commander-in-chief of the Tlascaltecan army. Diego de Ordaz fell in love with her; but Cortés determined to keep her for himself. Jicoténcal, commanded by the senate to make peace with Cortés, did so reluctantly; but he maintained a personal attitude of hostility and hatred toward the Spaniards. During the sojourn of the latter in Tlascala, there grew between Diego de Ordaz and Jicoténcal a David-

Jonathan type of friendship that was not shaken even when Ordaz, not knowing of Jicoténcal's passion for Teutila, confessed to the latter his own love for her. Cortés, aided by the traitor Magiscatzín, brought about the ruin of the family of Jicoténcal and the subjection of the Republic. He continued his crude attempts against the honor of Teutila even after her marriage to Jicoténcal, removing the slight difficulty of her married state by hanging her husband on a false charge. But the lady poisoned herself rather than submit.

The story is frequently raised to a plane of passionate loyalty to ideals of human justice. This ardor for liberty, kindness and fair dealing and the author's love of natural man, unspoiled by civilization, constitutes the principal artistic value of the work. Cortés was the tyrant, seducer, arch liar, "barbarous assassin" and "detestable monster."[1] The Spaniards, with the notable exception of Diego de Ordaz, were cruel and unjust to excess. Their whole campaign was based on lies and deceit. In his portrayal, the greed, envy, cruelty, ambition, violence, immorality, deceit and general depravity of the

---

[1]*Jicoténcal,* 1826, Vol. II, p. 240.

Europeans were no more extreme than the chastity, kindness, unselfish patriotism, honor, innocence and virtue of the Amerinds. The author made only one exception to his characterization of each group, Ordaz for the Spaniards and Magiscatzín for the Indians. Concerning the honor of the Tlascaltecans he quotes one of them as follows:

> Los más ancianos de Tlascala no han visto nunca una injusticia en sus gefes, ni jamás han oído una tradición que empañe la gloria de los que han gobernado la nación.[1]

Ordaz is glorified along with the Tlascaltecans. His use of physical force to escape from Doña Marina, who had lured him into her bedroom,[2] reminds one of Joseph's flight from Potaphar's wife and of Amadís de Gaula's attempts to protect his virtue.

The author's conviction that the natural state of man was admirable and that civilization had corrupted him is distinctly an echo of Rous-

---

[1] *Ibid.*, Vol. I, p. 67.

[The oldest men of Tlascala have never seen an injustice in their leaders nor have they ever heard a tradition that would stain the glory of those who have governed the nation.]

[2] *Ibid.*, Vol. I, pp. 135-136.

seau.[1] To him even the primitive superstitions
were better than the pious hypocrisy of the Europeans. From Chateaubriand he imbibed the
beauty of soul and nobility of spirit of the
Amerind; but there is in this work nothing of
the rich description of idealized nature found
in *Atala* and *René*. The only mention of natural
background is that of the woods in which Teutila sought refuge and that of Popocatépetl in
eruption.

There is a pronounced similarity between the
general trend of thought in parts of this novel
and that of Voltaire's *L'Ingénu*. The conversation
between Fray Bartolomé de Olmedo and Jicoténcal the elder, in which the wise old Amerind
confused the good priest with penetrating comments on Christian doctrine as preached by the
chaplain and as practiced by the soldiers, is
rather like the Huron's comments to the abbé
in *L'Ingénu*. Repeatedly one is reminded of the
attitudes of Voltaire.   Cortés, after receiving
with the priest a lesson on virtue from an Indian
woman, was almost persuaded to abandon his
tactics of criminal deceit and violence. When,
however, Olmedo added his sermon, urging

---

[1]Especially the *Discourse on Arts and Sciences*, 1749.

Cortés to heed the woman's advice, something insincere in the nature of the religious system represented by Olmedo broke the spell of good influence and Cortés remarked rudely: "To-morrow we go to Mexico." The author is herein fighting for a new interpretation of religion in which pure ideals of perfect goodness and universal love should replace institutionalized routine; an interpretation that would make of religion a synthesis of man's best aspirations, emotional and intellectual.

On another occasion Jicoténcal, after a confession of faith in the good God who is pleased only by goodness in his people, a faith far superior to anything Olmedo could claim for his religion, which permitted men to murder with God's approbation, remarked:

¡Gran Dios! . . . ¿ es posible tanta perfidia, y tanta doblez, y tanta falsedad, y tanto arte, y tanta infamia?[1]

Later the honest old man remarked:

---

[1] *Jicoténcal*, Vol. I, p. 185. Also p. 47 *et seq.* of Vol. II.

[Great God! . . .: are so much perfidy, so much duplicity, so much falsehood, so much subtle deceit and so much infamy possible?]

. . . es imposible que Dios se haga anunciar por medio de crimenes.[1]

When Father Olmedo told him that God had revealed His mysteries and miracles, the latter asked to be instructed in some elemental mysteries. When the ecclesiastic replied that they were impenetrable, Jicoténcal replied:

Luego Dios no ha revelado nada. ¿Y tú quieres hacerme creer que ese Ser, tan sabio, ha comunicado unas cosas que repugnan a mi razón? ¿Qué fin podría haberse propuesto en una conducta semejante? ¿El de probar tu sumisión a su voluntad: el de que reconozcas tu pequeñez y tu ignorancia? ¿Y qué necesidad hai (sic) para eso de unos misterios contradictorios y absurdos, cuando tengo mi juicio, que continuamente está midiendo mi flaqueza; y una voz que me dice aquí en el corazón que debo ser reconocido y obediente al Autor de todo bien? Mis deberes están bien claros; y cuando la miseria de mi naturaleza intenta estraviarme de su senda, tengo en mí un instinto, una cosa que me los recuerda, y que tú llamas razón: ¿Y quieres que yo renuncie a este gobernante para agradar a Dios? ¿Para qué me lo habría dado en este caso?[2]

---

[1]*Ibid.*, Vol. II, p. 48.
[. . . it is impossible that God should have Himself revealed through crime.]
[2]*Ibid.*, pp. 50-51.
[Then God has revealed nothing. And would you have me believe that that Being, so wise, has revealed things that are repugnant to my reason? And what end could He have had in mind in such con-

The discussion that followed emphasized the differences between practical Christianity and the complicated theoretical theology of that day. Olmedo's only answer was that miracles proved the correctness of his religion. Jicoténcal asked him to show him a miracle or, failing this, to tell him of one he had seen. The Amerind then added his conviction that a miracle was impossible and a belief in such was an affront to a wise and powerful God. He stated his belief that everything was governed by immutable laws, and demanded to know why it was necessary to interfere by miracles with plans made by an infinitely wise God.

duct? That of testing your submission to His will? That of having you recognize your smallness and ignorance? And in the accomplishment of that end what necessity is there for contradictory and absurd mysteries, when I have my judgment which is constantly measuring my weakness, and a voice that tells me here in my heart that I ought to be grateful and obedient to the Author of all good? My duties are very clear; and when the lowness of my nature would have me stray from the path they mark for me, I have in me an instinct, something that makes me remember them, something you call reason: and would you have me renounce this governing principle in order to please God? Why then did He give it to me?]

The perplexed priest took refuge in a recital of some of the beautiful teachings of Christ. to which Jicoténcal replied:

> Sin duda, mi amigo, esas reglas vienen de Dios; ellas están en mi pecho, y me las ha dado el mismo a quien debo estas manos, esta lengua con que te hablo, y los pensamientos que te espresa. Sí; yo siento, de la misma manera que siento el hambre y la sed, que es menester ser justo y benéfico; y esto lo sientes tú que vienes de regiones tan distantes, como lo sienten más de veinte naciones que pueblan el país que yo conozco. Tú eres más blanco que nosotros, tienes barbas y otras diferencias que al parecer te hacen un hombre de otra especie que la nuestra; y no obstante, tu moral es la misma que la mía. Luego ésta viene de Dios. Si quieres que yo adore este Dios contigo, dame ese manjar blanco que tú le ofreces; pues me es indiferente ofrecerle un poco de copal o cualquiera otra cosa, con tal que le manifieste mi reconocimiento.[1]

The Christianity of the Europeans was later characterized as

---

[1]*Ibid.*, Vol. II, pp. 54-55.

[Without doubt, my friend, those rules come from God; they are here in my heart, and they were given to me by the same one to whom I owe these hands, this tongue with which I speak to you, and the thoughts it expresses to you. Yes; I feel in the same manner that I feel hunger and thirst that it is necessary to be just and kind; and the same thing you feel, you who come from far distant regions, just as more than twenty nations who populate the country that I know feel it. You

> ... la monstruosa mezcla de las máximas más
> justas y más dulces con los hechos más atroces
> y más inicuos; y de los discursos más profundos
> y delicados con los absurdos más necios y desprecia-
> bles.[1]

Jicoténcal could not understand Olmedo's contention that criminality in the Christian fold
was better than virtue in any other.

Doña Marina, who had been baptized, renounced in a rage at the last the religion taught
her

> ... con la mentira, con la intriga, con la codicia,
> con la destemplanza, y sobre todo con la indiferencia
> a los crímenes más atroces.[2]

---

are whiter than we, you have whiskers and other
differences which seemingly make you a man of
different species from ours; and yet your moral
law is the same as mine. Then it comes from God.
If you want me to adore this God with you, then
give me that white morsel that you offer Him,
for it is of no importance whether I offer Him a
little copal or something else, so long as I manifest
to Him my gratitude.]

[1]*Ibid.*, Vol. II, p. 133.

[. . . the monstruous mixture of the justest and
sweetest maxims and the most atrocious and iniqui-
ous deeds; of the profoundest and most delicate
discourses with the most foolish and despicable
absurdities.]

[2]*Ibid.*, Vol. II, p. 134.

[. . . with lies, with deceits, with greed, with dis-

In one zealous onslaught against the Christian
regime the author has an Amerind say:

> ¡Tú el órgano de Dios! ¡Entre vosotros el ins-
> trumento de su palabra! ¡Hipócritas! Estáis llenos
> de vicios abominables, ¡y osáis suponeros los
> ministros de un Dios! No sé si el vuestro será
> algún ser tan maléfico y malvado que merezca
> semejantes adoradores; pero estoi segura que sois
> los verdaderos enemigos del que gobierna el mundo,
> porque éste es bueno por su naturaleza . . . No,
> estrangero, tú no conoces a Dios. ¡Un Dios, com-
> placerse en mi mortificación, sólo por la curiosidad
> de saber si yo soy sufrida! Si es el que gobierna el
> mundo, ¿qué necesidad tiene de pruebas para
> conocer una de sus ínfimas partes? ¿Ni qué le
> importa a su grandeza que yo me conforme o no
> con sus decretos. . . ?[1]

Jicoténcal was made to die comforted by assurance of reward for his just and virtuous life,
while Magiscatzín, who had gone over to the

---

order and, above all, with indifference to the most
atrocious crimes.]

[1]*Ibid.*, Vol. I, pp. 99-100.

[You the organ of God! The instrument of His
word among you! Hypocrites! You are full of
abominable vices, and you dare to suppose your-
selves to be the ministers of a god! I do not know
whether your god is some being so malevolent and
depraved that he merits such worshipers; but I
am sure that you are the real enemies of the One
that governs the world, for He is good by nature
. . . No, stranger; you do not know God. A god

Christians, died tormented by his conscience for crimes to which he was incited by them.

The writer frequently gives evidence of contact with the critical spirit of his age. He had Jicoténcal say on one occasion:

> Yo no concibo como pueda haberse creado el mundo, porque no concibo que de la nada pueda salir nada; y mi imaginación reposa cuando lo supongo tan antiguo como su Ordenador: tampoco concibo la bondad, sabiduría, justicia y poder infinitos, porque la idea de una cosa sin término no cabe en mi entendimiento.[1]

But the author's idealism was not limited to the field of religion. The ideals of political freedom and of individual liberty inspired him to eloquence in his interpretation of his characters

---

(able) to get pleasure from my mortification only because of curiosity to know whether I am patient! If He is the one who governs the world, what need has He of proof to understand one of its smallest parts? Why should it affect His grandeur that I conform to His decrees or not?]

[1]*Ibid.*, Vol. II, p. 49.

[I cannot conceive how the world could have been created, because I cannot conceive how anything can come out of nothing; and my mind is at rest when I suppose it as old as its Ordainer; neither can I conceive of infinite goodness, wisdom, justice and power, because the idea of anything without limit is beyond my understanding.]

and the forces at play around them. Partly from his hatred of monarchy and love of democracy came the reactions of the writer in favor of the Republic of Tlascala and against the invaders. It is quite clear that he was fighting, not so much the political battles of the time of Cortés as those between liberalism and authoritarianism of his own day. Like Voltaire's philosopher talking to the Syrian, placing the blame for war and destruction of happiness on

> ... those sedentary and slothful barbarians, who from their palaces give orders for murdering a million men and then solemnly thank God for their success.[1]

the author charged that tyrants need no excuse for their cruelties. To him the most moderate of them felt defeated if he could not exceed the Neros and the Caligulas.[2] He charged that European monarchs, intent on maintaining their brutalizing regimes, had attempted to destroy all information concerning the Republic of Tlascala.[3] He characterized them as assassins

---

[1]Quoted in Will Durant: *Story of Philosophy*, Garden City, N. Y., n. d., p. 233. Translation is Durant's.

[2]*Jicoténcal*, Vol. II, p. 198.

[3]*Ibid.*, Vol. II, pp. 168-169.

of liberty,[1] guilty of vile and base submission to those who sustained their crowns.[2]

Turning from his attacks on organized Christianity and monarchy, the author praised republicanism and discussed the basis of true liberty, contending that not all the blame for tyranny belongs to tyrants; a large part of the blame attaches to the people who submit to oppression. Political slavery, he contended, is the natural and just lot of a nation of cowardly spirit,[3] for liberty abandons those who are unworthy of it and who do not have the knowledge and courage to defend it.[4] Despicable he considered the social groups that, seeing the evil of tyranny, suffered it patiently.[5] Jicoténcal was made to teach that the spirit of a man worthy of freedom, a true republican, can never be made to accept domination.[6]

At the beginning of the second volume the author advises unity of the factions among the people:

---

[1]*Ibid.*, Vol II, p. 205.
[2]*Ibid.*, Vol. II, p. 184.
[3]*Ibid.*, p. 167.
[4]*Ibid.*, pp. 167-169.
[5]*Ibid.*, p. 178.
[6]*Ibid.*, p. 200.

> ... si amáis vuestra libertad, reunid vuestros in-
> tereses y vuestras fuerzas, y aprended de una vez
> que si no hai poder que no se estrelle cuando choca
> contra la inmensa fuerza de vuestra unión, tam-
> poco hai enemigo tan débil que no os venza y
> esclavice cuando os falta aquélla.[1]

It is difficult to resist the belief that this advice was meant for Mexicans of the nineteenth century.

From a literary standpoint this novel is mediocre. The tone is at times artificially sentimental, the description of characters is so general and vague that they appear mere abstractions, and the criticism of social forces is so scattered and lacking in logical arrangement that no definite unity exists. The author frequently abandons the novel and becomes an essayist. The work suffers by comparison with the costumbrista works of Manuel Payno. It must be remembered, however, that Payno wrote of his own time and

---

[1]*Ibid.*, p. 5.

[... if you love your liberty, unite your interests and your forces, and learn once for all that if there is no power that will not shatter itself when it collides with the immense force of your union, neither is there an enemy so weak that he will not conquer and enslave you when that union is lacking.]

could therefore describe in detail what he had seen, while the author of *Jicoténcal* was treating a period very far removed. Furthermore, *Jicoténcal* is a work meant to be a vehicle for the expression of ideals of abstract justice, truth and right, and not for the painting of prosaic minutiae of life among the Indians. This lack of basis for detailed treatment of customs was compensated by the possibility for unlimited use of creative fancy, but for such the author was ill endowed.

In addition to the sources already mentioned, the author used liberally the *Historia de la conquista de México* of Antonio Solís. From the *Brevísima relación de la destrucción de las Indias* by Fray Bartolomé de las Casas he took the spirit of opposition to the Europeans and love for the Amerinds, without, however, considering the latter as incompetent children as the venerable ecclesiastic had done. His work is akin to those of d'Arlincourt in one regard, the spirit of political mission, an element quite characteristic of nearly all Mexican historical novels.

The authorship of *Jicoténcal*, published in Philadelphia in 1826 remains an unsolved problem. Its inclusion here is necessarily tentative. Its importance goes beyond its intrinsic value because if it is Mexican, the historical novel appeared in Mexico before it did in Spain. But if the work is Spanish, it will be necessary to revise the date of the appearance of the historical novel in Spain. Professor William Zellers, who will soon publish the results of his investigation in the field of the Spanish historical novel of the nineteenth century, recently stated in a letter: "It is barely possible that this genre began before 1828, but it is impossible to prove it, as the work in question has long been out of print." For the present we shall have to leave the problem without solution.

El misterioso

The next historical novel to appear in Mexico was *El misterioso* of Meléndez Muñoz (1836), a work that merits little comment. It deals with the reign of Phillip II of Spain, especially the death of the unfortunate prince, Don Carlos. It contains little more than extravagant tales of crimes of personages that are too exaggerated and distorted to be convincing. There is neither effective creation nor formal refinement. The style and material are artless. Luis González Obregón places the work among the worst of the romantic school.[1]

JUSTO SIERRA

After Fernández de Lizardi the first known novelist of merit was Justo Sierra. He was born in Tixcacal Tuyú, Yucatan, September 24, 1814. Though of an old and illustrious line, his immediate family was not wealthy. He was educated in the *Seminario Conciliar de San Ildefonso* in the state capital and in the *Universidad Literaria de Yucatán*. In 1834 he received the degrees of Bachelor of Canon Law and Doctor of Scholastic Theology and Morals. Later he won the degree of Doctor of Laws. He held several responsible positions, including those of Secretary to Col. Sebastián López Llergo in the campaign against the centralists in Campeche, District Judge in Campeche, special envoy for his state in the conflict with the central government in 1841, *Consejero del Gobierno, Vocal de la Asamblea Departmental de Yucatán*, Deputy to the National Congress in 1852 and again in

---

[1]Quoted in Juan B. Iguíniz: *Bibliografía de novelistas mexicanos,* México, 1926, p. 217.

1857, and President of the *Academia de Ciencias y Literatura de Mérida*. He took a prominent part in the opposition to Santa Anna's centralist pretentions. His name appears on the decree of January 1, 1846, declaring the independent sovereignty of Yucatan.[1] He was prominent as a journalist throughout most of his adult life, having established *El Museo Yucateco*, and *El Fénix*.

In the last few years of his life he began the arrangement of his complete works including his *Proyecto de un código civil mexicano* (1859 and 1860). In the year of his death, 1861, he was made *Benemérito del Estado de Yucatán*, and was listed in the *Sala Rectoral del Instituto Literario de Campeche* in 1873. He was honored by the erection of a staue in the *Paseo de Montejo* at Mérida in 1906.

During his career as a student Justo Sierra had come into intimate contact with the ideas of Domingo López Somoza and of Don Pablo Moreno, two men who molded his thinking and determined his social, intellectual and critical

[1] The principal source for the information contained in this paragraph is Abreu Gómez: *Justo Sierra O'Reilly y la novela*, an excellent article in *Contemporáneos*, no. 35, April, 1931, pp. 39-73.

criteria. The former had been maestro in the court of Madrid, but was expelled for his liberal ideas in general and his progressive attitudes in legal matters in particular.

Don Pablo Moreno was Professor of Philosophy in the seminary in the state capital of Yucatan. The ambitious youths of the state came to consider him the representative of enlightened progressivism and looked to him for guidance. Among the most prominent of his disciples were L. de Zavala, Quintana Róo, and M. J. Solís. Zavala wrote of him:

> ... el primero que se atrevió a introducir la duda sobre las doctrinas más respetadas por el fanatismo.[1]

He waged war on the peripatetism of the theologians of his day and started a renovation along lines of modern philosophy.[2]   He fought the

---

[1] Lorenzo de Zavala: *Ensayo histórico de las revoluciones de México desde* 1808 *hasta* 1831, Vol. I, p. 45, and Eligio Ancona: *Historia de Yucatán,* Barcelona, 1889, tomo III, libro sexto, p. 13.

[... the first man who dared to introduce doubt concerning the doctrines most respected by fanaticism.]

[2] On one occasion he presented a student of philosophy against all comers in public discussion. The professors of theology who accepted the challenge were beaten and scandalized when the student refused to accept a statemen of Saint Thomas as a valid major prem-

fanaticism of his contemporaries, and scoffed at the seriousness of his orthodox opponents, attached, according to his conception, to their regime of childish superstition. So skeptical of dogma and of the whole social order of his time was he that he had to be disciplined for stoutly defending his heretical views. His attitudes did not change even after severe reprimands; but he was forced to cover his heresy with silence.[1]

It is not surprising that Justo Sierra absorbed liberal attitudes from his contacts with the ideas of these two great liberals. The influence of Domingo López Somoza is clearly discernible in Sierra's *Proyecto del código civil mexicano*, a study of legal affairs that has furnished the basis for the codification of civil laws of the Republic;[2] and the attitudes of Pablo Moreno appear in the critical analysis of religious institutions in *La hija del judío*.

---

ise. Moreno was ordered by Bishop Esteva to cease his liberal teachings. He soon retired from teaching and took up writing. Samples of his writings may be found in several of the newspapers of Yucatan published during his time, especially *El museo yucateco*. See also Chap. I, Vol. III, book VI of Ancona's *Historia de Yucatán*, Barcelona, 1889.

[1]Ancona: *Historia de Yucatán*, Vol. III, pp. 11-15.

[2]Iguíniz: *op. cit.*, p. 346.

The two novels of Sierra listed by Iguíniz are *Un año en el Hospital de San Lázaro* and *La hija del judío*. Torres-Rioseco gives the date of the first edition of the former as 1841. It appeared in the *Registro yucateco,* Vol. I, first issue, 1845. It was reprinted in Vol. 54 of *Biblioteca de Autores Mexicanos,* 1905.

Un año en el Hospital de San Lázaro was the first of a projected series of novels, the entire group to be called *Los filibusteros del siglo xix;* but the series was not continued. Abreu y Gómez mentioned the fact that Portillo y Rojas believed that Sierra got the idea for this work from *Los leprosos de Costa* of Xavier de Maistre.[1] It is not truly historical, though Sierra at first had planned to make it so by dealing with the history of piracy in the coast region. His plan was so indefinite that he quickly left the historical factors in a position of negligible importance and completed a thoroughly unsatisfactory story of an individual who had contracted syphilis. The reader cannot escape the feeling that the author was groping his way uncertainly.

La hija del judío was first published in *El*

---

[1]Abreu y Gómez: *op cit.,* p. 45.

Fénix, 1848-1850 over the anagram José Turrisa. There was an edition in 1874 containing a prologue written by Crescencio Carrillo y Ancona, Bishop of Yucatan, whose comments had as a general motive the softening of the charges brought indirectly by Sierra against religious institutions of the day. In 1908 it was published again in two volumes as part of the *Biblioteca de Autores Mexicanos.* There is a later edition that bears the date 1917.

The author begins this work with a convincing description of Merida, Yucatan. The house described existed in reality as he pictured it, but never in reality more convincingly than in his book. The pen picture of this house reminds one of Scott's careful descriptions of the setting for some of his novels. The story carries the reader to that house as it was in the middle of the seventeenth century when it was the home of Alonso de la Cerda, a citizen highly respected by all classes.

This gentleman and his wife had adopted María, a little girl whose family had been exterminated and its property confiscated by the Inquisition on the charge that her father was a Jew. As María approached her majority, the

Dean of the Cathedral and Commissary of the *Santo Oficio* demanded that she enter a convent lest she claim her parents' fortune and take it from that holy tribunal. The Jesuit priest, Prepósito, spiritual adviser of the young man with whom María was in love, took up the fight in favor of the young lady and saved her from the power of the Dean, partly through humanitarian motives and partly for a share of the young lady's fortune.

The battle of wits between the Jesuit and the Dean, the uncanny shrewdness of the former and his intelligent manipulation of the forces involved, political and ecclesiastic, are fully as interesting as the love story. Father Prepósito is the chief character of the novel, the quiet but powerful force that finally brings all others into subjection. He is a faithful representative of the best of his order, admirable for his learning and ability, but interested in the welfare of his order above every other consideration.

The Inquisition as an institution shares with the political corruption of the times the role of opposition. Its abuses of power created a reign of terror against which citizens were powerless. While Sierra was more interested in creative

art and less concerned with attack than many
authors who treated of the *Santo Oficio*, his
analysis is frank and unequivocal. His characterization of the Inquisition is quite evidently
what it should be in any work of art, not a documented attempt at historical accuracy, but an
artistic device for the achievement of his literary objectives. There is no interest in the Inquisition *per se* nor as the enemy of progressivism. The story demanded the use of that venerable institution in the role of obstruction and
oppression, and the author so used it. And he
used it well; for it hangs over the lovers like
the threatening hand of evil fate that constantly is on the point of crushing their hopes. The
lovers seem hopeless without the Sphynx-like
Jesuit, Father Prepósito, the mysterious master
detective who plays with their fate for his own
purposes long after he came into possession of
the means of saving them.

This dramatic conflict does not seem forced
and artificial. The action appears perfectly mo-
tivated and developments seem to be the natural
results of the causes in operation. And what is
more important still, the characters undergo a
literary resurrection that leaves them alive and

worthy of the reader's sympathy or opposition. There is here the type of naturalness that helps the reader to identify himself with the frustrated protagonist. Of abuses of exaggeration and cheap sentimenality, common to many Mexican historical novels, there is little in *La hija del judío.*

The style, like the progression of events, is quite logical, and is free from unnecessary ornamentation. The author was evidently dissatisfied with the serial form, however, for he wrote of the work:

> Tan incompleta y llena de incorrecciones como ha sido preciso publicarla, puede llegar a ser una cosa diferente cuando dándole toda la amplitud de que es susceptible, hagamos de ella una segunda edición... un trabajo que tanto merece limarse, y aún modificado no vale la pena todavía de circularlo suelto.[1]

Sierra never found time to make the corrections and alterations he contemplated. It was pub-

---

[1]*Biblioteca de Autores Mexicanos,* Vol. LXIII, p. vi.

[So incomplete and full of errors as it has been necessary to publish it, it may be much better when, giving it all the expansion the material merits, we print a second edition... a work that needs so much polishing and that even with modifications is not yet worth the trouble of publishing in serial form.]

lished in its original form by *La Revista de Mérida.*

In *La hija del judío,* for the first time in Mexican fiction, there is found a plot that makes a harmonious whole with its several sub-plots and achieves balance through close interlocking. In this regard it is superior to that of all other Mexican novels published up to that time. There are no loose ends as in the works of Lizardi and Payno. One of the attractive features of Sierra's plot mechanics is the mystery element that enters into the story, an element of which Sierra's predecessors were seemingly incapable.

Justo Sierra's knowledge of foreign works was so comprehensive that it is difficult to disentangle the influences that were brought to bear on him. Certainly he felt the appeal of the romantics from whom he learned the importance of interesting plot. Though in one instance he decried the habit of Bulwer-Lytton, Dumas, Sue, and Scott of presenting their heroines as perfect in beauty and grace,[1] these authors and Victor Hugo molded his ideas of plot. Bishop Carrillo Ancona's suggestion as to the influence of Sue and Victor Hugo, whom he called "patri-

---

[1]*Ibid.,* p. 10.

archs of horrible socialism" whose works were blacklisted by the church,[1] is well founded, though that influence was not so dire as the ecclesiastic thought.

If an artist deserves to live in proportion to the life he creates; if he deserves resurrection to the extent that he gives new life and meaning to facts that without his work would be meaningless or formless, Justo Sierra deserves continued life for the contribution he made to Mexican literature in *La hija del judío*.

In connection with *La hija del judío* it is in order to call attention to the fact that the Inquisition has been an important factor in other Spanish-American novels. After the suppression of that venerable institution it became the object of profound curiosity because of the mystery in which it had been wrapped throughout its existence. Furthermore, its stern official routine quite naturally had clashed sufficiently with individual interests to furnish an inexhaustible source of dramatic conflict.

In the five-year period between 1845 and 1850 there appeared in serial form in Chile a novel written by the Argentinan Vicente Fidel

[1]*Ibid.*, p. viii.

López, who was then a political refugee from his own country. This novel, *La novia del hereje, o la Inquisición de Lima,* deals with the interference of the Inquisition in a love affair between a Peruvian girl and one of Sir Francis Drake's officers. Using the heresy of the girl as a pretext, the officials of the Inquisition bring charges against her in the hope of confiscating her fortune. But the Englishmen, cast in the role of heroes, force the release of the girl and carry her away. One of the friends of the heroine becomes the wife of Sir Francis Drake and the principal love story ends with the marriage of the two lovers.

López stated in the *Carta-Prólogo* of his works that his desire was

> . . . poner en acción los elementos morales que constituían la sociedad americana en el tiempo de la colonización.[1]

López' opinion of the difference that should exist between formal history and the historical novel is evident in his statement:

> Así como de la vida de los hombres no queda

---

[1]Vicente Fidel López: *La novia del hereje o la Inquisición de Lima,* Buenos Aires, 1917, p. 14.

[. . . to set in motion all the moral elements that constituted American civilization in the period of colonization.]

más recuerdo que el de los hechos capitales con que
se distinguieron, de la vida de los pueblos no quedan
otros tampoco que los que dejan las grandes peri-
pecias de su historia. Su vida ordinaria, y por decirlo
así, familiar, desaparece; porque ella es como el
rostro humano que se destruye con la muerte. Pero
. . . el novelista hábil puede reproducir con su imagi-
nación la parte perdida, creando libremente la vida
familiar.[1]

The first Chilean novelist, Manuel Bilboa,
published in 1852 the story of two pairs of
lovers separated by the Inquisition. As in most
Spanish-American novels based on the Inquisition there is in this work, *El Inquisidor Mayor o
historia de unos amores,* a tendency to achieve a
sense of conflict by painting the inquisitors as
unscrupulous men using their official power for
their own selfish ends. The details of the death
of Moyen, one of the characters, add a note of
horror that is not uncommon in such works.

---

[1]*Ibid.,* p. 19.

[Just as of the lives of men there remains only
the memory of the outstanding actions by which
they distinguished themselves, of the life of a
people there persist only those memories that great
crises drag in their train. Its ordinary life and, so
to speak, its intimate life disappears; because it is
like the human face which death destroys. But . . .
the good novelist can reproduce with his imagination the lost features, creating freely the more
familiar aspects of life.]

Los dos hermanos is a sequel to *El Inquisidor Mayor*. It continues the story of the attempt of one inquisitor to marry the beautiful wife of his victim. But during the marriage ceremony the lady's husband appears on the scene and forces the corrupt official to take his own life.

To the group of Spanish-American novelists of the nineteenth century who dealt with the Inquisition belong two other Mexicans, Juan Antonio Mateos and Riva Palacio. From the archives of the Inquisition in Mexico Riva Palacio gathered material for two novels, *Monja y casada, virgen y mártir* and *Martín Garatuza*, the latter being a sequel to the former. Genaro García is authority for the statement that "the most valuable part of the archives of the Inquisition of Mexico" belonged to Riva Palacio's private library.[1] Material from this source was used freely in the two novels cited. In *Las dos empedradas, memorias de la Inquisición*, the Inquisition appears but it does not play so important a role as the subtitle would indicate.

Juan A. Mateos used the Inquisition to good

---

[1]Genaro García and Carlos Perreyra: *Documentos inéditos o muy raros para la historia de México*, México, 1906, V. first sentence of the *advertencia*.

advantage as a force of opposition in *Sacerdote y caudillo.* In this novel he presented in an interesting and convincing manner the attempts of the *Santo Oficio* to bring about the downfall of Hidalgo, the revolutionary leader. Though the Inquisition is referred to several times in the course of *Los Insurgentes, continuación de sacerdote y cauldillo,* it plays no important part except in the fate of Morelos, who fell victim to its authority.

Further discussion of the works of these two Mexican novelists will be found later on in this dissertation.

Though they were not novelists, two men should be mentioned in connection with the novelists who wrote about the Inquisition, Ricardo Palma and José Toribio Medina.

Among the works of the famous inventor of the literary type evidenced in *Tradiciones peruanas* is a series of sketches on the Inquisition published in 1863 under the title *Los anales de la Inquisición en Lima,* covering the activities of the Inquisition from 1570 to 1820. In this series the author used the same general procedure as in his well known *Tradiciones peruanas,* a spicy revitalization of historical episodes.

José Toribio Medina has made what is probably the most exhaustive study of the Inquisition in America ever published. Appointed secretary to the Chilean legation in Lima, he spent much time studying the archives kept there, gathering material on history and literature. While examining the archives at Simancas, Spain, he learned that many of the records of the Inquisition in America were there. On the documents found in Lima and Simancas he based his published works on the Inquisition. The information he furnished has been of value to literary men seeking to recreate the past.

MANUEL PAYNO

In 1845 Manuel Payno began the publication of *El fistol del diablo* in *La Revista Científica y Literaria*. There was an edition published in 1859, another in 1871, one in 1906 and one in 1917. The length of the novel may be seen in the fact that the 1871 edition was published in four volumes of 443, 407, 419 and 383 pages respectively- a total of 1641 pages. It is a rambling story without logical progression, having no definite plan, no sense of direction or proportion, very little unity and much material that is de-

cidedly not germane. The influence of Fernández
de Lizardi is quite evidently responsible for
most of these weaknesses. In justification of
Payno it can be said that his defects are not so
annoying as those of Lizardi, the only Mexican
model he had, for he does not have the air of
amateur preacher that mars *El Periquillo Sarniento*. Payno's preachments are tempered with
a calmness born of experience and intellectual
maturity.

The plot of *El fistol del diablo* is its weakest
aspect. Beginning with a pact-with-the-devil device, the story drifts rather than progresses
through a maze of episodes. The author at first
planned to have the story unified by the magic
scarf pin that passed through the hands of
many characters; but finding difficulty in fus-
ing the fantastic factors with his realistic purpose, he seemingly abandoned all attempt at
unity, and more through lack of sense of direction than by definite plan, completed a series
of pictures of Mexican life loosely connected
by an unconvincing and pointless story. Payno
himself remarked concerning this work:

> . . . no es realmente una novela, sino una serie de

escenas reales y positivas entre personajes que han existido, y aun existen.[1]

It is significant that he made this statement in the epilogue of the second volume as a criticism of the finished work rather than in the preface to the first volume. He realized that his work was lacking in plot mechanics, and that its procedure was quite too unsophisticated to justify its unqualified classification as a novel; but he was aware that in its *costumbrista* phases it had merit. His statement is at once an apology for the former and a recommendation of the latter.

The recommendation is not less in order than the apology, for the work contains some striking descriptions and type studies. The influence of the works of the Spanish *costumbristas,* especially those of José de Larra, on this work is clearly discernible. Payno's frank analysis, his satire and his insistence on common sense as a guide in social and political matters were learned from Spanish authors of the period. His best pictures are not surpassed in faithfulness

---

[1]Manuel Payno: *El fistol del diablo,* tercera ed., Vol. II, p. 1051.

[... it is not really a novel, but rather a series of real and actual scenes among people who have lived and still live.]

to realistic detail. The tone is not that of the usual reformer inspired by zeal for some cause; there is evident at times a mild cynicism and aloofness that are in contrast with the ultra-seriousness of his contemporaries, just as his clarity and plainness differ from the perorative tone of many of his fellow countrymen of the nineteenth century.

As early as chapter four, type pictures of Mexican society of unquestionable realism appear. Rugiero reveals to Arturo the character and motives of all the individuals gathered at a fashionable ball: the capitalist, made rich by cruelty to unfortunates and by flattering governmental officials; the general, decorated for bravery, though in battle he always contrived to stay out of the danger zone; the old magistrate, using his authority as his avarice and concupiscence dictated; the rich society matron, deceiving her husband and corrupting her daughter; foreign diplomats, protesting their love and admiration for Mexico while detesting the nation heartily with a feeling of their own superiority; women kissing each other with protestations of affection though their inner hatred incited them rather to biting each other. The commentator's imputation of motives to the guests is reminiscent of Lucrecia's thrust at Celestina: "You do nothing except for selfish reasons." He concluded with the statement:

> Nunca hay más enemistad entre la sociedad que cuando, como ahora, espléndida y brillante se reúne al parecer para divertirse, pero en la realidad para especular y aborrecerse.[1]

In discussing Mexico's condition in general, Rugiero, the Devil, remarked in a slightly cynical tone that as long as outrages and immorality were tolerated from the governor's palace to the humble home, and from the highways to the highest officials, Mexico could not have lasting stability.[2] This comment differs essentially in tone from like comments made by Lizardi in that it was made by the devil who was not interested in reform, rather than by an author actuated by zeal for reform and renovation. The difference is decidedly in favor of Payno.

In these descriptive and critical digressions the author discovered his strength. From that

---

[1]*Ibid.*, Vol. I, p. 81.

[Never is there more enmity in society than when, as now, splendid and brilliant its members gather, apparently to amuse themselves, but in reality to observe and abhor each other.]

[2]*Ibid.*, p. 80.

point to the end of the work the plot is a mere
frame for pictures and commentaries that reveal almost every phase of Mexican life. He
described the dirty slums of Mexico City, without sidewalks, with unpaved streets into which
refuse water drained and formed puddles that
filled the air with their stench; the dirty dwell-
ings and their scant furnishings;; the unfortunate human herds vegetating in filth;[1] the house
of the wash-woman, used as a meeting-place for
lovers;[2] the gambling dives and their clien-
tele;[3] the medical practices of the day;[4] travel
in stage coach;[5] the tactics of highway bandits,
and the cowardice of federal soldiers in conflicts with robbers.

Few institutions escaped analysis. The poli-
ticians and their made-to-order armies, the judicial organization, the police system and the
church are all reviewed. Of the first the author
remarked:

[1]*Ibid.*, pp. 88-89.

[2]*Ibid.*, pp. 125-127.

[3]*Ibid.*, Chap. xxvii. This is very similar to a description in *Los bandidos de Río Frío*, 1928, Vol. II, pp. 242-
249.

[4]*Ibid.*, p. 216.

[5]*Ibid.*, Chaps. xiv and xv.

Los altos personajes que decían *mi pueblo* y *las masas* se procuraron, de grado o por fuerza, aguadores, cargadores de la esquina, borrachos de la pulquería, sirvientes domésticos que no cabían en ninguna casa, vagos de los barrios y algunos indígenas de los pueblos, y con todas estas masas formaron su guardia nacional. Los vistieron con uniformes de colores, largos y anchos, cortos y estrechos; los armaron con fusiles un poco mohosos y sucios, y comenzaron a tocar retretas y dianas y a gritar: ¿Quién vive? en las altas horas de la noche, apenas pasaba un perro descarriado o un gato en busca de su novia.[1]

These high personages played, ate, received favors and good salaries, and occupied the highest places for the sake of *mi pueblo;* they made a motto of *religión y fueros,* especially the latter; they were the parasitic class who talked loudly of patriotism and religion when their

[1]*Ibid.,* Vol. II, p. 627.

[The high personages that were habitually saying *my people* and *the masses* gathered, by fair means or by force, watercarriers, porters from street corners, drunken sots from pulque shops, domestic servants who were useless in any household, vagabonds from the slums and Indians from villages, and with all these they formed their national guard. They dressed them in brilliant uniforms, long and wide, short and narrow; they armed them with dirty and rusty guns, and these soldiers began to shout "Who goes there?" in the dead of night every time a stray dog passed or a cat ran by in search of its mate.]

only interest was to protect their special privileges.[1] This same group refused to pay its debts to veterans of the war for independence while dressing newly appointed political militarists in costly finery.[2]

With biting severity Payno ridiculed the police force, which, with the corrupt judiciary, fostered rather than discouraged crime and public degradation. In one instance he resorted to exhortation in Lizardi's style, formally directing more than two pages to public officials.[3] He was no less severe with the judiciary. A judge before whom a girl was hailed on a false charge of stealing a diamond pin remarked to himself: "Either the girl or the diamond will be mine."[4]   Beautiful women, even though innocent of the charges, could gain their liberty only by favors to the judge or to the jailor;[5] and men, likewise by favors, but of a more economic kind.

In *El fistol del diablo,* Payno's strong aver-

[1]*Ibid.,* Chap. xxxvii.
[2]*Ibid.,* Vol. I, p. 105.
[3]*Ibid.,* pp. 89-92.
[4]*Ibid.,* p. 197.
[5]*Ibid.,* Chaps. xix and xx.

sion to prisons of the kind then in existence and his advanced conception of criminology led him into interesting portrayals of prison life. The entire regime he branded as uncivilized and unmoral; and he contended heatedly that the purpose of punishment should be the restoration of the criminal to a decent normal role in society, or, failing this, the orderly and humane segregation of the incorrigible. But in Mexico he saw only the primitive procedure of crushing the accused even before his guilt was established, depraving his soul and alienating him permanently from decent living.[1]

All of Payno's wrath was unleashed on the operators of women's prisons, with their indecencies and with the intrigues of the jailors and clerks to force the attractive girls to consort with them, isolating select ones on the pretext that they were dangerous to the other women in order the better to attain their purpose with threats and promises.[2] He complained that public bailiffs merited more punishment than the prisoners[3] and reminded the proud liberals that

---

[1]*Ibid.*, p. 278.
[2]*Ibid.*, Chaps. xix and xx
[3]*Ibid.*, p. 527.

their prisons were worse than the dungeons of the Inquisition.

The list of legal deficiencies and abuses treated directly or indirectly is too long to be included. Those presented are enough for our purpose. It should be added, however, that in them Payno found the symptoms of an ailing society not yet ready for inclusion under the term civilization as he conceived of it.

Contemporary political history assumes importance in some chapters. The troublesome problems of the property of the church, the church's role in politics,[1] and in general, the conflict between the liberal and conservative factions are all brought to the foreground. Payno is severe in his treatment of the clerics. He stated that:

> ...los clérigos a su vez se quieren servir del pueblo, explotando su fanatismo e inclinándolo a una guerra religiosa.[2]

Into the mouth of one in sympathy with the conservatives he puts the words:

---

[1]*Ibid.*, Vol. II, Chap. XL.

[2]*Ibid.*, p. 658.

[The clergy in its turn tries to exploit the public, making capital of its fanaticism and inciting it to religious strife.]

> Entre los clérigos no reina más que la hipocresía
> y el obscurantismo, y los retrógrados que los dirigen
> nos volverían de buena gana a la Inquisición.[1]

A penetrating examination of the foibles of leaders, especially religious leaders, is found in Father Martín's soliloquy.[2] But Payno discounted the tendency to charge clerics with all of Mexico's ills. One of his most beautiful charactors is a devout priest.[3] He denied the accuracy of certain romantic tales concerning the Inquisition.[4]

Most of the abuses so far mentioned Payno considered as results, not as causes, of conditions existing in Mexico. As the chief cause he cited the lack of unity among the classes. He confessed with shame that foreigners had ground for calling Mexico uncivilized when they saw how the lower class lived and was treated. He expressed faith in the *léperos*, contending that they were the products of forces beyond their

---

[1]*Ibid.*, Chap. XL, p. 657.

[Among churchmen there reign only hypocrisy and obscurantism, and the retrogrades that govern them would gladly return us to the Inquisition.]

[2]*Ibid.*, pp. 704-706.

[3]*Ibid.*, Vol. I, pp. 283-284.

[4]*Ibid.*, Vol. II, p. 736 in footnote.

control, and that they needed only an economic role to develop into respectable citizens.[1]   Of the basic character of his fellow countrymen he said:

> ... somos charlatanes, versátiles, apasionados y apáticos aún en las cosas del propio interés; olvidamos con facilidad los agravios, sin perdonarlos, y no tenemos energía para llevar a cabo nuestras resoluciones.[2]

In Mexicans he saw a people dominated by constant thought of conspiracy, unable to see their social obligations and to interest themselves in hard work and in their families.[3]

The first volume of *El fistol del diablo* is not strictly a historical novel. While the general background is so evidently that of the second quarter of the nineteenth century that the reader can link occasional incidents with definite historical events, the connection is quite indirect. The material of chapter XLVII of the second vol-

---

[1]*Ibid.*, Vol. I, p. 91.

[2]*Ibid.*, p. 696.

[... we are charlatans, fickle, intolerant and apathetic even in things that affect our own personal interest; we forget easily insults without pardoning them, and we do not have the industry to carry out our resolutions.]

[3]*Ibid.*, p. 525.

ume, however, has a historical basis almost in its entirety. The last part of the second volume is likewise definitely historical, dealing with the period immediately preceding the war with the United States and continuing to the autumn of 1847.[1]

Much of the material of *El fistol del diablo* can be traced to the author's experience in public affairs and to his contacts with foreign institutions and cultural attitudes. From early youth he was almost contantly connected with some department of the government. In 1842, at the age of thirty-two, he was named secretary to the Mexican legation in South America. His duties in this position carried him to Europe. He spent much of his time there traveling through England and France, studying literature and the history of institutions with such success that he was able later to write some interesting short stories on various episodes of English history. Soon after his return from Europe he was commissioned to study the penal system of the United States. Both *El fistol del diablo* and *Los bandi-*

---

[1]This date is established by the mention of the battle of Cerro Gordo (see Vol. II, Chap. LV and incidents that occurred the night of September 15, 1847 (see *Ibid.*, p. 1032.)

dos de Río Frío reveal his interest in and knowledge of modern penology, a part of which was learned from study of practices in foreign countries, especially in the United States. As indicated in the criticism of those two works, much of Payno's careful depiction of all aspects of criminology in Mexico is traceable to the study made in the United States and the stimulus furnished thereby for further study in his own country.

But not all of Payno's knowledge and inspiration came from political science and related materials. The emphasis placed on details of customs and environment by the *costumbrista* writers of Spain had appealed so strongly to him that he accepted their technique. It is not too much to say that Payno's works are of most value in those parts in which he followed the lead of that group, for his pictures of customs and descriptions of national types constitute a veritable recreation of a society of a given epoch.

El fistol del diablo is lacking in the patriotic zeal that pervades much of the composition of Juan A. Mateos and Riva Palacio. Payno's unemotional and realistic viewpoint led him to accept the good and condemn the evil of all political and social groups. His consistent refusal to assume a fixed and fervid loyalty to any party left his judgment clear for objective evaluation of forces at play around him. The lack of subjective force of which this aloofness is indicative is reflected in *El fistol del diablo*.

This objective attitude is at once an advantage and a weakness. It enhances the authenticity of his pictures of the scenes involved and gives the author greater claim to consideration as a reliable critic of social affairs; but it imposes severe limitations upon emotive forces that result in artistic creation. Payno's work is more photographic than creative.

In 1861 Payno published *El hombre de la situación*, a novel of 249 pages. Everything of value in the work could be put in ten pages of description of colonial life in Mexico. The story is a weak attempt at imitation of some of the better known picaresque novels.

In 1871 there appeared a collection of Payno's short stories under the title *Tardes nubladas*. On the whole, they are lacking in literary merit. There is almost nothing of the sparkling realism of his two most important works, and the style is often that of holiday peroration.

The story called *La lámpara* is an adaptation of material taken from Thierry's *Récits des Temps Merovingiens*. *Pepita* is a short historical story of the epoch of independence, too full of artificial sentimentality and rhetorical inflation to be of value, and *El castillo del Barón d' Artal* is no better. *El poeta y la santa* is a translation of a historical narrative by Thierry, for whose "fluid and agreeable style" Payno expressed admiration.[1] The third story of the group is *Isabel de Inglaterra*, an unimportant fragment of eight pages, in which the only significant fact is the evidence of Payno's admiration for Walter Scott, whose *Kennilworth* he thought excellent. *Granaditas* deals with the capture of Guanajuato by the forces of Hidalgo. In it the figures Riaño, Pipila and Hidalgo are sublimed after the manner of Juan A. Mateos.

The most interesting of the group from the standpoint of naturalness and sincerity is *Un viaje a Vera Cruz en el invierno de 1843*. It is

---

[1]Manuel Payno: *Tardes nubladas,* Mex. 1871, p. 139, footnote. Thierry was a disciple of Chateaubriand, influenced especially by *Les Martyrs* of the latter.

a travelogue with historical narration about the places of interest on the journey.

The descriptions, though not polished literary pictures like those of Altamirano, are quite vivid. It has some of the good points of *Los bandidos de Río Frío.*

María Estuardo reaches a length of ninety-two pages. It is a well balanced, attractive and convincing account of the life of Mary, Queen of Scots. Putting aside the question of the historicity of Payno's story as irrelevant in a discussion of literary values, the reader observes in this narrative the author's ability to win for his character the sympathy that attaches to all personages of the past who have been given true resurrection at the hands of a true artist. The language is unobtrusive, but adequate for narration of the simple type attempted. The work has more unity than either of Payno's long novels, probably because the author had a better conceived plan than in the latter.

This work was the outgrowth of Payno's visit to the British Isles and of rather extensive reading. There is internal evidence that he had read *Kennilworth, The Abbot* and *The Monastery,* all three by Scott; the published correspondence of

Queen Mary; the works of Agnes Strickland, of Hume, of Smollet and of Aikens, and Prince Labanoff's collection of documents concerning Mary's execution. He gives evidence of skill in the manipulation of the information gained from these sources.

In the first volume of an anthology called *Episodios históricos de la Guerra de Independencia* Payno has five historical stories on subjects indicated by the title of the collection, and several in the second volume. It is hard to believe that the author of *El fistol del diablo* and of *Los bandidos de Río Frío,* in which such a calm tone is maintained, could be the author of some of these stories. There is here an inflamed passion for his country, a release of the subjective to its limit. The heroes of the fight for liberty become epic saints sublimated in an attempt to escape from human limitations into a realm of perfect ideals. As was the case with many other Mexican historical novelists, Payno's flight into idealistic interpretation forced his characters to gravitate, each toward one of two opposite poles, perfect goodness or utter depravity. There is present, however, too much suggestion of holiday oratory to leave an impression of genuineness of emotion.

JUAN DÍAZ COVARRUBIAS

This unfortunate author was born in Jalapa in 1837. After his father's death in 1846 he was carried to Mexico, and three years later was enrolled in the *Colegio de San Juan Letrán*. His chief interests as a student included the humanities, philosophy and medicine. The War of Reform drew him into the ranks of the liberals as a military doctor. He and several of his youthful companions were captured and executed in 1859, a scant four months after his twenty-first birthday.

From early childhood Díaz Covarrubias had given evidence of unusual literary ability; but destiny closed the path before him. He wrote the following: *Impresiones y sentimentos, La clase media, Gil Gómez el insurgente, o la hija del médico, La sensitiva,* and *El diablo en México.* Though none of these works can be called great, it is remarkable that during a period of strife a mere youth should produce two even mediocre novels, one of which has had five editions and the other two.

The only one that concerns us here is *Gil*

Gómez el insurgente o la hija del médico, published first in 1858. There was an edition in 1859, two in 1902 and one in 1919.[1]

Gil Gómez was an orphan living in the home of an estate owner in Yucatan. The latter had a son, Fernando, who was in love with Clemencia, daughter of a doctor who lived close by. When the revolution of 1810 became imminent, Fernando left home to join the royalist forces. Gil Gómez attempted to follow him, but came by accident to the town of Dolores on September 15, 1810. After spending the night in the house of Hidalgo he was so impressed with the latter's character that he decided to stay with him.

A woman who lived in the capital hated the revolutionists to the extent that she promised to give herself to a nobleman, Don Juan, if he would kill Hidalgo. After several of Don Juan's attempts to assassinate the venerable revolutionist were frustrated he finally succeeded in delivering him into the hands of the viceroy's

---

[1] The edition of the *Biblioteca de Autores Mexicanos,* published in 1902 and the 1919 edition contain a biography of the author written by Villaseñor y Villaseñor.

officers. The woman who had given her word
to Don Juan then tried to escape the necessity
of meeting his demands that she keep her bar-
gain, by inciting Fernando to kill him. The
latter, who was in love with the woman, conquered Don Juan. His victim, seeking revenge,
lay in wait to kill him, but was prevented from
doing so by Gil Gómez, who appeared in time
to save him. Gil Gómez and Fernando then returned home to find Clemencia, the doctor's
daughter, dying of grief over the indifference
of Fernando.

This work is decidedly mediocre. The story
is burdened with artificial sentimentality and
loses its tone of sincerity because of unnatural
formal decorations. Gil's zeal for the revolution
is improbable in the light of the reason for his
departure from home, and his appearance at
the right time to prevent the assassination of
Hidalgo and Fernando makes him appear as a
guardian angel. The love affair of Fernando
and Clemencia and the story of Gil Gómez are
in artificial juxtaposition in the story.

CHAPTER III

FROM THE REFORM MOVEMENT TO THE BE-GINNING OF REALISM.

In the late fifties there began a struggle without possibility of compromise between two opposite points of view, the liberal and the reactionary. The heat of that struggle separated the population into two camps, both radical in their attitudes and bent on extermination, each unaware of its own weaknesses. Mexico was a nation seething with hatreds, wherein moderation scarcely existed. In that period every fireside was a forum for fierce outbursts; all eyes were blinded by swirling storms of passion, and all ears were filled with the roar of fanaticisms. But for the first time in Mexican history the issue was clearly defined and understood, and for the first time the liberals had a clear conception of their own program.

It is significant that the outstanding leaders of the liberals were Indians and *mestizos*, representatives of the majority of the population, and that the reactionaries were creoles forming themselves around the church as a nucleus.

Speaking in general of conditions in Mexico during that period, and in particular of the in-

efficiency of the republican group, Jesús Agras
exclaimed:

> ¿Qué es y ha sido México desde el gran día de su
> independencia? . . . el pueblo más desgraciado de la
> tierra . . . Víctima sucesivamente o de la ciega tira-
> nía militar o del desenfreno de la demagogia, ni un
> solo día ha disfrutado los goces de una verdadera
> sociedad. . . todas y cada uno de los mexicanos. . .
> han visto irse destruyendo hasta extinguirse todo
> aquello que forma el atractivo de la vida social.[1]

He charged that Mexico was worse than a no
madic society, for in the forests at least people
would not be plagued with

> . . . una mentida civilización, los odios, las vengan-
> zas, las miserias, las pasiones todas, en fin, de una
> reunión monstruosa sin leyes eficaces, sin autoridad
> verdadera, sin obediencia, sin moralidad pública y
> sin amor procomunal.[2]

---

[1]Jesús Agras: *Reflecciones sobre la naturaleza y
origen de los males y trastornos que han producido la
decadencia en México,* etc. Guadalajara, 1864, p. 7.

[What is Mexico and what has she been since the
great day of her independence? . . . the most unhappy nation on earth . . . The victim successively
either of blind military tyranny or of the license
of demagoguery, not for a single day has she en-
joyed the fruits of a true society . . . every Mexican
has seen everything that contributes to the attractiveness of social life destroyed.]

[2]*Ibid.,* p. 7.

[. . . the false civilization, the hatreds, the vengeance, all the passions . . . of a monstruous hoard
without efficacious laws, without true authority,

One of the most damaging bits of testimony concerning society in Mexico in that epoch is the statement of the Empress Charlotte:

> Your majesty perhaps believes, as I did, that nothingness is incorporeal; on the contrary, in this country one stumbles upon it at every step, and it is made of granite, it is more powerful than the spirit of man, and God alone can bend it . . . one has to struggle against the wilderness, the distances, the roads, and the most utter chaos.[1]

Altamirano protested that literary gatherings were of no interest to people, the theatres were unattended, except by the few who had no other way to escape from the sight of the poverty, degradation, filth, and prosaic barbarism of the human ant-hill. The capital he thought melancholy, anemic, with the squalor, nakedness, indolence, starvation and abysmal depravity of the proletariat overbalancing the attractions of *El Zócalo* and *Plateros* Avenue. The social functions of the higher class were stagnant. There was neither initiative nor variety, even among the leaders of society who held their

---

without discipline, without public morality and without public loyalty.]

[1]Egon Caesar Corti: *Maximilian and Charlotte of Mexico,* N. Y., Knopf, 1929, Vol. II, p. 469.   See also p. 422.

roles by divine right rather than by merit. There were no critics, only eulogizers.[1]

Such conditions could not stimulate or even support literary production. Juan Díaz Covarrubias, aware of the futility of writing for such a public in such stressful times, wrote to Luis G. Ortiz:

Tal vez habrá muchos que digan que sólo un niño o un loco es el que piensa escribir en México en esta época aciaga de desmoronamiento social, y pretende ser leído a la luz rojiza del incendio y al estruendo de los cañones.[2]

Though, as previously stated, education in Mexico was in general still ineffective at the time of the Reform movement, in fact was to continue so to be throughout the century, there had developed a group of thinkers and teach-

---

[1] I. M. Altamirano: *Paisajes y leyendas*, pp. 131-148.

[2] Juan Díaz Covarrubias: *Obras completas*, on the first page of the dedication of the first novel in the collection. The date of the anthology and the title of the first story are both missing in the copy found in the García Collection.

[There will perhaps be those who will say that nobody but a child or a crazy man would think of writing in Mexico in this unfortunate period of social disintegration, and hope to be read by the red glow of incendiarism and to the accompaniment of roaring canons.]

ers whose love for liberalism amounted to religious ardor. This group, beginning with Ignacio Ramírez, the intellectual whip of his generation, and including such men as Ignacio Manuel Altamirano and Justo Sierra, did more to renovate Mexican society and literature than all other educational agencies combined; in fact they constituted the only progressive factor in education.

Ramírez, widely known by his pseudonym *El Nigromante*, while still a student showed his rebellious and independent temperament by defending the thesis "There is no God; all animate nature is self-sustaining." That heretical pronouncement was not the prattle of an undisciplined student; it was a declaration of war against practically all traditionally consecrate attitudes on the part of one of the sharpest intellects Mexico has produced. As an orator, as a journalist, and as a teacher, Ramírez became the implacable destroyer of everything associated with the old regime. He became the guiding spirit of a group of young intellectuals into whose minds he planted ideas that constituted the basis of the reform movement.

As the mentor of liberalism Ignacio Ramírez

represented the tardy application of a true cosmopolitanism to the social problems of Mexico. Though his attitudes were stimulated largely by extensive reading of foreign literatures, they were not the uncritical products of that reading. That he had only disdain for the superficial liberalism that manifested itself in the repetition of catch phrases taken from superficial foreign thinkers is shown by such statements as the following:

Devoramos en las ciencias a los vulgarizadores enciclopédicos, sin notar que no son extensos en sus tratados, sino porque son superficiales.[1]

He was unerring in his diagnosis of Mexico's intellectual ills as results of ignorance and undigested erudition.

The ideals of Ramírez and of his disciples systematized the movement for reform and culminated in the Constitution of 1857 and the Reform Laws, the two most important achievements of Mexican history in that they laid bare

[1]Ignacio Ramírez: *Obras*, México, 1889. Sec. de Fomento, Vol. I, p. 351.

[We devour in the sciences the works of encyclopedic quacks, without noticing that they are not extensive in their treatises, but because they are superficial.]

the basic ills of the nation and pointed out the road to progress.

With Benito Juárez, the exponent of the political ideals of this group, we have little to do here; but of Ignacio Manuel Altamirano, the literary preceptor of his generation, we must take account at the proper time, for it was he that indoctrinated Mexican writers in literary nationalism and became teacher and personal adviser to a whole generation of amateur novelists and poets.

ELIGIO ANCONA

Eligio Ancona was born in Mérida, Yucatan, in 1836. He studied law at the *Universidad Literaria del Estado*. Like many other literary figures of Mexico, he was prominent in political affairs, serving as governor *pro tem.* of his native state, judge in a circuit court, judge of the Supreme Court of Mexico, and as deputy to the national congress. As a journalist he used the columns of *La Píldora* and *Yucatán* in defense of the liberal cause against the regime instituted by the imperialists. He was recognized by the learned societies of his time as one of Mexico's important erudites. His contribution to the history of Yucatan is largely contained in his *Historia de Yucatán*.

Acona wrote six novels, of which five are historical: *La cruz y la espada* and *El filibustero*, 1866; *Los mártires del Anáhuac*, 1870; *El Conde de Peñalva*, 1879; and *Memorias de un alférez*, published in 1904, eleven years after the author's death. All of these historical novels have two volumes each except *El Conde de Peñalva*.

El filibustero is the story of Leonel, an orphan left in infancy on the doorstep of D. Gonzalo Villagómez, a rich *encomendero* of Valladolid. D. Gonzalo and his wife, doña Blanca, loved the child as if he were their own until the birth of a daughter, Berenguela, four years later; then they grew strangely cold toward him.

Leonel learned rapidly under the instruction of Father Hernando of the Franciscan convent of Sisal and became the self-appointed tutor to Berenguela. The two fell in love; but their plans to marry met the determined opposition of D. Gonzalo and his wife, who had arranged Berenguela's marriage to a nobleman. Leonel challenged his rival to a duel, but instead of fighting him attempted to save him from a mob. In the confusion the fiancé of Berenguela was killed and Leonel was wounded.

Intent on keeping the two lovers separated, doña Blanca and Father Hernando had Leonel thrown into prison. When the latter was released he learned that Berenguela had married. He left home and became a pirate, assuming the name Barbillas.

In one of his raids the pirate Barbillas and his men captured the Captain General of the provine of Yucatan and several political dignitaries traveling in his company, among whom was the husband of Berenguela. Later, when Berenguela was free from her husband, Leonel wanted to marry her. Father Hernando, his old teacher, imprisoned the girl in a convent; but in the face of the threat of Leonel to take her by force the friar revealed to him that his lover was in reality his half sister, for Leonel was the son of Father Hernando and doña Blanca.

Leonel in desperation visited a man unjustly condemned by the Inquisition to prison for the remainder of his life, exchanged clothes with him and permitted him to escape, taking thus on himself the sentence he allowed the other to avoid.

The story is somewhat emotional in tone. In one case it was said of Leonel:

> El se llevaría aquel cadáver que nadie había visto, escogería un rincón ignorado del mundo para sepultarlo, construiría junto a la tumba una cabaña, y allí al lado de Berenguela ... conversando diariamente con ella, esperaría tranquilo y feliz el fin de sus días.[1]

Other traces of romantic subjectivism are apparent in the violence of reactions, in extraordinary situations, in the mystery surrounding the origin of the chief character, in the interest in the distant past, in the resort to piracy, and in the manipulation of plot for the sake of effect. Berenguela is like the typical romantic heroine, beautiful, helpless, and self-effacing; Leonel is the perfect lover driven by desperation to piracy.

There is in this work a tendency to give free reign to fancy in the manner of dealing with historical facts. Historical accuracy was wisely

---

[1]Eligio Ancona: *El filibustero,* 1866, Vol. II, p. 328.

[He would carry away that corpse which nobody had seen; he would choose an unknown corner of the world in which to bury it; he would build a cabin close to the tomb, and there at Berenguela's side ... talking to her every day, he would await serene and happy the end of his days.]

rejected as a criterion by the author. His aim was creation within a very loose framework of historical trends. Characters such as he presented in this work never existed except in his fancy, but they had real existence there.

The author, furthermore, capitalized his personal reactions to the institutions of the colonial regime to add effectiveness to his interpretation. Those institutions and their personnel furnished the element of difficulty or dramatic conflict in the story. Justice and virtue are augmented in attractiveness by such descriptions of their opposites as the following:

> Al valiente conquistador... ha sucedido el indolente encomendero que ... sólo cuida de explotar al miserable indígena.
>
> Al celoso misionero ... ha sucedido el fraile o el cura convertido en publicano, que gasta la mayor parte de su tiempo en inspeccionar el cobro de sus rentas.
>
> A los grandes aventureros ... han sucedido los gobernadores y capitanes generales, que con muy honrosas excepciones sólo se dedican a sacar de su posición toda la utilidad posible.[1]

---

[1]*Ibid.*, Vol. I, pp. ii-v.

[The valiant *conquistador* has been succeeded by the indolent landholder whose only interest is the exploitation of the natives.

The zealous missionary has been supplanted by

There is something of pathos in his description of his own native state of Yucatan as one of the most unhappy places of Spanish America, partly because of its subjection to repeated attacks of pirates who established their base at Belice.

The author injected something of the holy zeal of a crusader into his attacks on the Inquisition and on ecclesiastical organizations in general. These were developed in the role of opposition to the realization of the legitimate aspiration of the chief characters. Without concerning ourselves with the accuracy of his characterization, the reader can accept the depiction for artistic purposes. Whether fair or not, Ancona's satire and ridicule are part of the effectiveness of the story. Especially indicative of his use of these literary tools is his treatment of the customs of honoring saints with bull fights, and of trying men before the Inquisition on charges of being Mohammedans because they

---

the friar and the priest turned publican, who spends most of his time overseeing the collection of dues.

The great adventurers have been followed by governors and captains general, who, with honorable exceptions, dedicate themselves to wresting from their positions all the gains they can.]

never drank wine,[1] and on charges of being
Jews because they bathed themselves and
changed clothes on Saturday. The latter charge
was brought against the innocent Cifuentes by
a priest's niece, with the result that Cifuentes
was found guilty and sent to prison. Ancona related with convincing indignation that the goods
of heretics were accursed, that their possessions
would corrupt any Christian except the inquisitors themselves.[2] He included in this story a
rather vivid description of the Inquisition's instruments of torture and the use to which they
were put.[3]

An interesting manifestation of Ancona's zeal
to find virtue and value in unsanctified places
and to uncover conventionalized abuses among
official spokesmen of authoritative bodies is
seen in the statement he put into the mouth of a
pirate:

> ... esa sociedad perversa en donde el hermano
> vende al hermano, en donde el que debe proteger os
> sacrifica a sus infames pasiones, en donde las más
> dulces y las más santas afecciones ceden a la

[1]*Ibid.*, Vol. II, p. 171.
[2]*Ibid.*, pp. 202-203.
[3]*Ibid.*, pp. 199-200.

insaciable codicia del oro o al vil influjo del poder.[1]

In the formation of his interest it was natural that Ancona feel the influence of his famous fellow-townsman, Justo Sierra. Not only did Ancona absorb much of Sierra's interest in the history of Yucatan, but he was the first Mexican novelist to follow the lead offered in *Un año en el Hospital de San Lázaro* by writing a novel based on the pirates that infested the coast of Yucatan. So strongly was he impressed with Sierra's use of colonial history as a field for the novel that three of his stories deal with the same generation as *La hija del judío*. Leaving out Payno's *El hombre de la situación*, Ancona's *El filibustero* is the first full length novel after Sierra to deal with the pre-independence period; and, counting *Jicoténcal* as a Mexican novel, it is the third Mexican novel to deal with that epoch.

Ancona owed more than general fields of in-

---

[1]*Ibid.*, p. 228.

[... that perverse society in which brother sells brother, in which the one whose duty it is to protect sacrifices you to his vile passions, in which the sweetest and most saintly affections give way to insatiable greed for gold or to the evil influence of power.]

terest to Sierra; he was indebted to his prede-
cessor for his zeal for liberal institutions and his
antagonistic attitude toward the old regime. The
Inquisition assumes in Ancona's work much the
same aspect and role as in *La hija del judío*. The
same is true of other institutions and of conditions in general in the province of Yucatan. But
Ancona is more subjective than Sierra; his attacks against the colonial regime are more direct. His portrayals are interesting; indeed *El
filibustero* is of interest even to the reader of today.

In the same year that *El filibustero* was published there appeared another historical novel
of Ancona under the title *La cruz y la espada*, in
two volumes of 296 and 312 pages respectively.

Four years later, in 1870, he published his
Los mártires del Anáhuac in two volumes of 326
and 322 pages respectively. Since writing *El
filibustero*, Ancona had acquired a more definite conception of the technique and material
of the historical novel. In *Los mártires del Anáhuac* the progression of the story is more logical, the plan is clear and is more carefully followed, and there is less to offend one's sense
of reality. Out of the mass of details connected

with the conquest of Mexico Ancona chose a few and developed them in such a manner as to leave a clear impression of the significant aspects of the struggle.

Because Ancona emphasized the importance of Cortés' strategy in utilizing the dissidence existing among the Amerinds rather than attributing the success of the invader to superhuman bravery and prowess, the novel has more verisimilitude than the accounts of some of the professional chroniclers of the conquest. It gains in plausibility by attributing much of the success of Cortés to the internal disintegrating forces that had destroyed the solidarity of the Aztec empire before the coming of the Spaniards. Cortés' genius stands out more clearly in the dextrous manipulation of local forces than in superhuman military exploits.

His success was made more natural by the fact that the superstitious Amerinds, bewildered by the horses and cannons of the invaders, and restrained for some time by the belief that Cortés was the returned spirit of Netzahualcoyotl, delayed their resistance long enough to permit the invader to win for himself the support of some influential local leaders.

So natural and inevitable does the course of events seem that the reader is almost prepared to agree with the Aztec priests that the gods had decreed the destruction of Anáhuac; and that the strange beared invaders were merely catalytic agents, intrinsically insignificant, furnishing only the impetus for the long and tragic processes of reduction. Ancona utilized this situation in creating a dramatic sense of impending doom, with the bearded captain playing constantly the role of villain and hero. The entire work has a good balance of dramatized history and novelistic elements.

In no other Mexican historical novel is the reader made to sympathize with both the contending forces so much as in this one. The daring band of Spaniards, led by a brave adventurer into the territory of a people capable of crushing them with an army of a quarter of a million men, excites admiration; and the intrepidity shown in the burning of their only means of escape is a true epic not surpassed by the exploits of all the imaginary knights of literature. Yet sympathy of Cortés is tempered by a like feeling for the Amerinds, superstitious, defeated by themselves and threatened with the

most humiliating fate ever experienced by a
people. Their grief for Anáhuac is like the la-
ment of the Jews over the fall of Jerusalem:
"By the waters of Babylon we sat down and
wept," and like the song of the Babylonians:
"Babylon is fallen, is fallen to rise no more."
The reader is made to regret that the proud race
was to be swept into the ignominy of practical
slavery and spiritual annihilation.

But not all is admiration and sympathy. The
Amerinds are despicable at times for their weakness and cowardice, and Cortés changes his role
from that of hero to that of cruel and treacher-
ous schemer, then back to that of hero. He is at
once a genius of unsurpassed bravery and a
monster of inhumanity, admired and hated by
the reader.

There are a few contradictions in the story;
for example, in relating the story of Tizoc's
father the author has the Aztecs furnish beautiful maidens for the enjoyment of the sacri-
ficial victim during the period of preparation
for the sacrifice. This fornication is sanctioned
by the priests and by the people; but later, sex
irregularity is branded as the most heinous
crime in the eyes of the Aztecs and their gods,

punishable by crushing the heads of the guilty parties. Gelitzli, the daughter of Montezuma, whom Cortés violated after giving her a powerful drug, was cursed forever by the gods; and although she was not a willing party to the act, the people determined to sacrifice her.

The chronology is not always accurate. But the discrepancies the work contains are few and not serious, for Ancona was quite familiar with the general facts of the conquest and subsequent domination. In this story the author has aided popular appreciation of the basic social forces involved, and what is more important, has used the historical background as materials for an interesting bit of literary creation.

By pointing out the fact that the introduction of Christianity into Mexico was aided greatly by the similarity between the religion of the Amerinds and Christianity, Ancona creates a feeling of the basic similarities of human aspirations of all races, however widely dispersed. Some of the factors of each are pathetic, some are admirable; but in essence they are all human and therefore similar. Both emphasized the device of pleasing God by the infliction of suffering on human beings, especially on those considered to be enemies or heretics. In both religions that sacrifice at times went to the extreme of taking human life. The author does not descend to the plane of polemics by attempting to show the fallacies of one and the credibility of the other; he uses both to build his situations as his purposes demand.

Missing entirely the beauty of symbolism of Christian ceremonies, the aborigines had no difficulty in substituting the statues of saints for their idols and the various members of the Holy Family for their deities. Santiago, the patron saint of warriors, fitted into the place of Huitzilopochtli; San Isidro, the patron of harvests, was easily confused with Matlacueye and Centectl. Even the idea of the Trinity caused the Amerinds no trouble, its acceptance being a matter of changing names.[1]

The system of *encomiendas* and *repartimientos* is described as a device conceived for the protection of the natives but one that resulted in their practical enslavement. It was a Don Quijote who had left the shepherd lad in the hands of Juan Haldudo for protection.

[1]Eligio Ancona: *Los mártires del Anáhuac*, México, José Batisa, 1870, Vol. I, p. 60.

The style of *Los mártires del Anáhuac* is not attractive; it is common-place, distinctly inferior to that of the better Spanish novelists and to that of Altamirano. Indeed its lack of variety and sparkle would render a less interesting plot quite boresome.

Several of the characters are well drawn and convincing; especially is this true of Cortés and Moteuczoma. The Spanish soldiers, fired by zeal for adventure and gold, the Amerinds, astonished and bewildered, both European and native made cautious by superstition, all are interesting as literary characters.

Concha Meléndez calls attention to the fact that *Los mártires del Anáhuac* is the first Mexican novel based on the conquest,[1] but acceptance of her statement must be deferred until the authorship of *Jicoténcal* is definitely established. The latter work, however, was probably unknown to Mexican authors of the latter half of the century. The Cuban, Gertrudis Gómez de Avellaneda's *Guatimozín* (Madrid, 1846 and Mexico, 1853 and 1857) had acquired considerable popularity, however, and was still wide-

---

[1] *El libro y el pueblo*, 1932, Vol. X, No. 5, p. 12.

ly read at the time when Ancona was writing
Los mártires del Anáhuac .

Las memorias de un alférez, published in
Mérida in 1904, is a historical novel dealing
with the attempts of a minor official of the
Spanish army stationed in Yucatan to solve the
mystery of the murder of the Captain-General
of the colony. His activities brought him into
conflict with the family of the girl he loved.

The plot is weakened by useless manipula-
tions, v. gr., in one instance the protagonist was
captured in a forest, bound, gagged, blindfolded and searched by a group of assassins
who then disappeared, leaving him alone. Later
they returned, searched him again, carried him
a little farther into the woods and left him. The
work abounds in unusual actions and situations.
It is not entirely plausible that the protagonist
should fall casually in love with a woman connected with those who were scheming to kill him,
nor that without knowing her name, station or
family he should call her "the one whom I loved
most in all the world" twenty-four hours after
seeing her for the first time.[1] Neither is it nat-

---

[1]Eligio Ancona: *Memorias de un alférez,* 1904, Vol.
I, p. 124.

ural that a letter found in the drawer of an old desk should be torn by chance in all the places that contained names and other data that could clear up a murder mystery. The reader cannot be expected to believe that a total stranger should be sufficiently interested in a local murder scandal to become terror-stricken, have his heart action impeded and his hair raised on his head by reading a letter written by the murderers, who probably would never have written such an incriminating document in the first place. And surely no sane man would be so indiscreet in the face of threats of death from a secret enemy as the protagonist was.

The work does contain, however, some interesting recreation of the epoch involved. Attention is called to the scarcity of books in the province as the result of censorship and import restrictions.[1]   The author compares the forces of justice to degenerate Roman nobles equipped with shields and steel swords fighting blindfolded slaves armed with wooden weapons.

Occasional statements reveal the author's tendency to seek the cause for attitudes and actions, for example:

---

[1]*Ibid.*, Vol. I, p. 60.

... pero es tan hermoso desempeñar el papel de redentor.[1]

... ese egoísmo de la naturaleza humana que tiende a buscar en otras personas el origen de las desgracias que acaso nos acarreamos con nuestra propia imprudencia.[2]

... El valor en el hombre se halla en razón directa de la salud que disfruta.[3]

Ancona incorporated into this work a few paragraphs on the primitive state of man and the delights of freedom in the wilds of nature that sound much like Rousseau's writing.[4]

La cruz y la espada, 1866, a story of the love of Alonso de Benavides and Doña Beatriz, into which Zuhuy-Kak, the daughter of an Amerind king is injected, contains practically all of the abuses of the early historical novels of Spain

---

[1]*Ibid.,* p. 36.

[... but it is so thrilling to assume the role of redeemer.]

[2]*Ibid.* p. 32.

[... that egoism of human nature which tends to seek in others the origin of the misfortunes which we perhaps bring on ourselves by our own imprudence.]

[3]*Ibid.,* p. 39.

[... Courage exists in a man in direct ratio with the health that he enjoys.]

[4]*Ibid.,* p. 146.

and France. Benavides wounded his lover's father while trying to elope with her. After the young man fled to America, Doña Beatriz followed him disguised as a man. She appeared in time to save him from the Amerinds, who were in the act of sacrificing him on a stone altar. Zuhuy-Kak had fallen in love with Benavides; but she was killed by an Amerind woman in order to prevent her marriage to a Spaniard. Benavides' troubles were removed when he learned that Beatriz' father was not her father at all and had desisted from his attempts to keep the two lovers apart.

There are evidences of poor imitation of Cooper and of Chateaubriand, and an abundance of illogical imagination. Even the life of the Amerinds, which might have saved the work from complete oblivion if it had been well portrayed, has no appeal, even in fancy. It, along with the plot, lacks the semblance of reality that is necessary even in a fantastic work.

El Conde de Peñalva is an historical novel published in 1879; but it is not available for study. Though *La mestiza*, 1891, is not historical, its emphasis on the conflict between the whites on one hand and the Amerinds and *mes-*

tizos on the other is in keeping with Ancona's preoccupation with the indigenous racial spirit.

IGNACIO MANUEL ALTAMIRANO

Ignacio Manuel Altamirano was born in Tixtla, in what is now the state of Guerrero, December 12, 1834. His family, of pure Indian stock, was given a Spanish name by the Spaniard who baptized them. The poverty common to Indians of Mexico was no stranger to Altamirano. González Obregón remarked that the boy lived to the age of fourteen like all Indian boys, ignorant, speaking only the tribal dialect of his people, untamed and occupied only with hunting and childish combats.[1]

Ignacio Manuel's father was elected *alcalde* of the little village. This distinction aroused in the local schoolmaster an interest in the boy's education. Then Manuel started on his remarkable career as a student.

By virtue of his excellence, demonstrated in competitive examinations, he won a scholarship

---

[1] The facts presented in this biography were taken mainly from González Obregón: *Noticia biográfico*, in *Biblioteca de Autores Mexicanos*, Vol. XXI, pp. v-xv, México, 1899.

that intitled him to free instruction in the *Instituto Literario de Toluca.* In 1849 he took up the study of Spanish, Latin, French and philosophy in that school. His abilities engenered respect for him among his teachers and fellows to such an extent that he was made librarian of the school.

González Obregón considers the contact with books given him by his duties as librarian one of the most important influences of his career, for "there it was that he fed his soul on knowledge and erudition."[1]

The sharp-witted scourge of authoritarianism and obscurantism in Mexico, Ignacio Ramírez, noticing this young Indian seated often outside the door of his classroom listening to his lectures, invited him in. The fiery liberalism of the teacher was the orienting force in the early attitude of the student.

Later Altamirano was given board and room at a private college in Toluca for his services as teacher of a class in French. But he was poor and impatient. He became a wanderer, trying his hand at teaching and even at production of

[1]*Ibid.*, p. vi.

a mediocre dramatic work, *Morelos en Cuauhtla,* which he had composed.

He entered the *Colegio de San Juan Letrán,* but his work was interrupted in 1854 by participation in the revolution. Though he was a good soldier, he realized that he was more of a student than a military man and soon resumed his study of law with the ambition of reforming the legal codes and the political machine. But even this was not enough to occupy all his attention. He became the leader of a group of young journalists interested in general social reform and in the improvement of literature. His private room became "the editorial office of a newspaper, a reformist club and a literary center which grew with the attendance of numerous students and partisans of the revolution."[1]

His role as teacher of Latin brought him a close acquaintance with classical literature from which emanated much of his grace and good taste.

When the Congress met in 1861, after the War of Reform had stirred anew the political

---

[1] *Ibid.,* pp. viii-ix.

passions of the nation, Altamirano went to that body as a deputy. When the amnesty bill came up for discussion, Altamirano, who had already acquired fame as an orator, asked for recognition on the floor. The effect of his speech is known to most school children of Mexico today. As an example of oral eloquence it has no superior in Mexican literature.

After the triumph of the liberals under the leadership of Benito Juárez, Altamirano, Ignacio Ramírez and Guillermo Prieto founded *El Correo de México*. (González Obregón is authority for the statement that Altamirano had already founded *El Eco de la Reforma* and *La Voz del Pueblo* in the state of Guerrero.) He and Manuel Payno established *El Federalista*, *La Tribuna* and *La República*, the directorship of which he gave up in 1881.

In 1869 Altamirano founded *El Renacimiento*, a weekly literary magazine of considerable influence in the development of literary trends of the latter half of the nineteenth century. Altamirano was editor of *El Siglo xix*, *El Monitor Republicano* and *La Libertad*. He contributed generously to *El Domingo*, *El Artista*, *El Sema-*

nario Ilustrado, El Federalista, El Liceo Mexicano and many provincial and foreign magazines.

But Altamirano's activities did not stop here. He was the center of several literary societies. He revived the defunct *Liceo Hidalgo*, was Secretary and Vice-President of *La Sociedad Mexicana de Geografía y Estadística*, founded the *Sociedad Gorostiza* composed of dramatic authors, was President of *Escritores Públicos* and of the *Sociedad Netzahualcoyotl*. He was a member of many foreign scientific and literary societies.

In political circles Altamirano was prominent, serving at various times as Fiscal de la Suprema Corte de Justicia, Procurador General de la Nación, Oficial Mayor de la Secretaría de Fomento and deputy to the National Congress.

In the field of education he was Professor of Administrative Law in the National School of Commerce, Professor of General and Mexican History in the School of Jurisprudence and Professor of Philosophy in the last named institution. In the latter part of his life his chief interest was education. "Leer y enseñar, y conversar sin descanso: tales fueron sus últimos afanes;

los libros y la juventud, sus fieles amigos y sus hijos predilectos."[1]

In 1889 Altamirano was appointed Mexican Consul General in Spain. Later he held the same post in France, having exchanged places with Manuel Payno because of his poor health. He died in San Remo February 13, 1893.

López Portillo y Rojas pronounced Altamirano's *Clemencia* the best Mexican novel of its time.[2] It was written after the author's return from the military campaign described in the work, a campaign in which he himself had taken part.[3] It is an expansion of a story Altamirano told one night to a group of ladies who later insisted that he put it in novel form. The first chapter appeared in *El Renacimiento* in 1869 as a part of *Cuentos de invierno*, and the remainder followed in the same magazine in serial form. In the same year Díaz de León y Santiago White

---

[1]Ignacio Manuel Altamirano: *Obras,* in *Biblioteca de Autores Mexicanos,* Vol. XXI, México, 1899, p. xiii of *Noticia biográfica.*

["To read and to teach, and to converse without ceasing; such were his greatest desires; books and youth, his faithful friends and his favorite sons."]

[2]Portillo y Rojas: *La novela. Breve ensayo, México,* 1906, p. 46.

[3]*Ibid.*

printed a very attractive second edition with good photographs by Cruces y Campa and with several excellent drawings. The popularity of the second edition was so great that it was sold in a few days. *Clemencia* was later reproduced in serial form by the *Grand Journal de Pérou,* a French-Spanish newspaper of Lima. The fourth edition was printed by Mr. Armas, director of a New York illustrated newspaper called *El Ateneo,* in the first volume of his paper. The fifth edition is that which appeared with *Las tres flores, Julia,* and *La navidad en las montañas* in a collection called *Cuentos de invierno,* printed by F. Mata in Mexico in 1880. Another edition appeared in Mexico and in Paris, no date, and still another in Valencia, no date.

The setting of the story is the region around Guadalajara in December, 1863, the year of the French occupation of Mexico. The historical material serves only as a frame for the actions of two officers in the army of the republic, one handsome and with an unusual appeal for women, talented and cultured, but at heart a coward and traitor; the other unattractive, but diligent, loyal and decent. A conflict developed over the affections of a beautiful woman, with a none too pleasant result.

The characterization of the four chief personages is well done, but the most attractive features of the work are the depiction of natural scenery and the pleasing style. There is a tone of genuine artistic dignity that contrasts sharply with the perorative style of most Mexican authors of the times. The fact that occasional excesses of inflated language creep in does not destroy the general impression of artistic discretion and sincerity. It is not too much to say that this novel and others of Altamirano incorporate the best aesthetic judgment and balance to be found in the Mexican novel up to the dates of their respective compositions.

In his narrative the author knew only one vein, that of constantly serious narration in which everything conforms to the sweet sadness of his temperament. At times the effect could be heightened if he had shed his seriousness long enough to relieve the strain.

He could not escape a constant preoccupation with the sense of tragedy of human life, the melancholy that was a part of his racial heritage and that made romanticism so attractive to him and his compatriots.

Altamirano's genius was too short of flight to create full-length novels, and he lacked the organizing ability necessary to present his excellent material in impressive plots. As a result, his works are little more than short stories. But his poetic genius gave a magic touch of life to nature and laid bare the beauties of the realm beyond superficial facts of the world and human nature. It is on this penetration into the soul of things that his fame is based. His was no surface world, but one of beauty hidden from the eyes of the unworthy; and he succeeded in painting that world with beauty and grace.

Altamirano's influence in the novel was primarily that of a preceptor who illustrated his teachings with short models. His stories were too few and too scant of plot to serve as complete novels; but his teachings gave encouragement and orientation to an inexperienced generation of writers, many of whom, however, needed much more than advice.

Altamirano sensed the increase of interest in literature that followed the fall of the empire of Maximilian and attempted to turn that interest into national channels. In the press, with which he was closely connected throughout his long career, in the classroom, from the lecture platform and in gatherings of literary men he preached consistently that Mexican authors should apply the best technique of universal art to Mexican life with the interpretation of the soul of their country as an ideal. Something of his spirit of patriotism may be seen in the following statements quoted from one of his critical essays:

¿Acaso en nuestra patria no hay un campo vastísimo de que puede sacar provecho el novelista . . . ?

¡Oh! si algo es rico en elementos para el literato, es este país, del mismo modo que lo es para el minero, para el agricultor y para el industrial.

La historia antigua de México es una mina inagotable . . . Los tres siglos de la dominación española son un manantial de leyendas poéticas y magníficas . . .

Nuestras guerras de independencia son fecundas en grandes hechos y en terribles dramas. Nuestras guerras civiles son ricas de episodios, y notables por sus resultados . . .

Nuestra era republicana se presenta a los ojos del observador interesantísima . . .

¿Y el último imperio? ¿Pues se quiere además de las guerras de nuestra independencia un asunto mejor para la epopeya? . . . Este pueblo mísero y despreciado, levantándose poderoso y enérgico, sin

auxilio, sin dirección y sin elementos, despedazando
el trono para levantar con sus restos un cadalso
. . .[1]

But not only in Mexican history did Altamirano see a field rich in material for the writer;
in the country's natural scenery and in its picturesque human types he saw an inexhaustible
field that had scarcely been touched. He de-
plored the fact that since the days of Fernández

---

[1] I. M. Altamirano: *Revistas literarias de México,*
México, 1868, pp. 9-10 and 12-13.

[Is there not perchance, in our country a vast
field from which the novelist can profitably draw
materials?

Oh! if anything is rich in material for the writer,
it is this country, just as for the miner, for the
farmer and for the industrialist.

The ancient history of Mexico is an inexhaustible
mine . . . The three centuries of Spanish rule are a
veritable spring of poetic and magnificent legends.

Our wars of independence abound in great deeds
and terrible dramas. Our civil wars are rich in
episodes and notable for their results.

Our republican era is exceedingly interesting to
the observer.

And the last empire? Does one wish in addition
to the wars of our independence a better subject
for epic literature? This people, miserable and despised, arousing itself, powerful and energetic, without help, without direction and without equipment,
destroying the throne to raise from its debris a
scaffold . . .]

de Lizardi and Manuel Payno Mexican writers
had neglected this richest of all sources of inspiration. He called attention to the progress
that had been made in other important Spanish
American countries, where writers

> Cantan su América del Sur, su hermosa virgen,
> morena, de ojos de gacela y de cabellera salvaje. No
> hacen de ella ni una dama española de mantilla, ni
> una *entretenue* francesa envuelta en encajes de
> Flandes.

> Esos poetas cantan sus Andes, su Plata, su
> Magdalena, su Apurimac, sus pampas, sus gauchos,
> sus pichireyes; trasportan a uno bajo la sombra del
> ombú, o al pie de las ruinas de sus templos del Sol,
> o al borde de sus pavorosos abismos o al fondo de
> sus bosques inmensos, ... le hacen ... escuchar el
> rugido de sus fieras terribles ... y meditar a orillas
> de sus mares. . .[1]

---

[1] *Ibid.*, p. 14.

[They sing their South America, their beautiful
virgin, dark with gazelle-like eyes and luxuriant
hair. They make of her neither a Spanish lady with a
mantilla nor a French entretenue wrapped in Flemish lace.

Those poets sing their Andes, their River Platte,
their Magdalena, their Apurimac, their pampas,
their gauchos, their *pichireyes;* they transport one
to the shade of the *ombú* tree, or to the foot of the
ruins of the temple of the sun god, or to the brink
of their awe-inspiring abysses or to the depths of
their immense forests, or they make him hear the
roar of terrible wild beasts and meditate on the
shore of their seas.]

As is to be expected, Altamirano saw as the chief obstacle to the proper development of this national material the habit of imitating slavishly the European models with which Mexico was flooded. He did not go to the extreme of advocating lack of attention to foreign literature; indeed he insisted that the literature of the older civilizations must be taken as a guide in the acquisition of good taste.

> No negamos la gran utilidad de estudiar todas las escuelas literarias del mundo civilizado; seríamos incapaces de este desatino, nosotros que adoramos los recuerdos clásicos . . . No: al contrario, creemos que estos estudios son indispensables; pero deseamos que se cree una literatura absolutamente nuestra, como todos los pueblos tienen, los cuales también estudian los monumentos de los otros, pero no fundan su orgullo en imitarlos servilmente.[1]

He expressed profound respect for such masters of the novel as Walter Scott, Cooper, Richard-

---

[1] *Ibid.*, pp. 14-15.

[We do not deny the great profit of studying all literary schools of the civilized world; we would be incapable of such folly, we who adore the memory of the classics . . . No; on the contrary, we believe that these studies are indispensable; but we wish for the creation of a literature entirely ours, like all peoples have, each of which also studies the literary monuments of the others, but does not base its pride on servile imitation of them.]

son, Dickens, Hugo, Balzac, and Dumas, and considered the study of their works essential to any novelist.

But he contended that foreign works were valuable to Mexican writers only for instruction in the general procedure and technique of composition, and not as sources whose materials were to be imitated. The author's attitude in this regard is best expressed in his own words:

> En cuanto a la novela nacional, a la novela mexicana, con su color americano propio, nacerá bella, interesante, maravillosa. Mientras que nos limitemos a imitar la novela francesa, cuya forma es inadaptable a nuestras costumbres y a nuestro modo de ser, no haremos sino pálidas y mezquinas imitaciones, así como no hemos producido más que cantos débiles imitando a los trovadores españoles y a los poetas ingleses y a los franceses . . .[1]
>
> Nosotros todavía tenemos mucho apego a esa literatura hermafrodita que se ha formado de la

---

[1]*Ibid.*, p. 13.

[As for the national novel, the Mexican novel, with its distinctively American color, it will be born beautiful, interesting, marvelous. As long as we limit ourselves to the imitation of the French novel, whose form is inadaptable to our customs and to our spirit, we shall produce only pale and mediocre imitations, just as we have produced only weak poetry while imitating Spanish, English and French poets . . .

mezcla monstruosa de las escuelas española y francesa en que hemos aprendido, y que sólo será bastante a expulsar y a extinguir la poderosa e invencible sátira de Ramírez, que él sí es tan original y tan consumado como habrá pocos en el nuevo continente.[1]

Altamirano called attention to the recent tendency toward expansion of the novel to such a degree that it had become a medium for the presentation of historical facts, intellectual and moral viewpoints, philosophical positions, and social, political, and religious propaganda.[2] It had come to be "the best vehicle of propaganda."

Reasoning from his major premise that morality is the most desirable characteristic of any people,[3] and from his contention that the novel was the school of the people, he came to the conclusion that the chief duty of the novelist is to

---

[1]*Ibid.*, p. 14.

We still have much fondness for that hermaphrodite literature which is made up of a monstruous mixture of the Spanish and French schools in which we have learned, and which can be expelled and extinguished only by the powerful and invincible satire of Ramírez, who is indeed as original and as nearly perfect as few others in the New World.]

[2]*Ibid.*, p. 29.

[3]*Ibid.*, p. 38.

guide the masses in the formation of virtuous and wholesome attitudes. Hence, the novelist was to concern himself with teaching patriotism, chastity, industry, honesty, and order. In this connection he cited the success that had attended the church's policy of indoctrinating the public by an educational program adapted to the ends it sought, and advocated the pursuit of the same policy by the novelist.[1]

Granted the wisdom of the procedure of the church in religious instruction and the fact that art does have a moral mission to perform, such advice given to unseasoned writers of a nation without literary orientation and experience had some unfortunate results, as will appear in the examination of many subsequent works whose authors were dominated by the desire to indoctrinate their fellow countrymen. It was easy for writers of an immature society to substitute superficial conventionalities for the deep moral principles Altamirano had in mind. By morality he meant what Plato meant when he used the word; but unfortunately, not all of his followers had the philosophical background necessary for a complete understanding of its true nature.

---

[1]*Ibid.*, pp. 70-72.

But in spite of his views concerning the duty of the novelist to indoctrinate, he persisted in his demand for impartiality and careful study of facts.

> En las novelas de costumbres se necesita tan grande dosis de fina observación y de exactitud, como para las novelas históricas se necesitan instrucción y criterio. De otro modo sólo se producirán monstruosidades ridículas. . .[1]

Statements concerning Altamirano's contribution to Mexican literature as critic and guide of his own and the following generations abound in the works of historians of Mexican literature. Morena Cora wrote concerning him:

> Altamirano más que ningún otro escritor ejerció grande influencia en la juventud estudiosa de su patria.[2]

Jiménez Rueda wrote:

> Poeta, novelista, maestro, ejerció en su tiempo

---

[1]*Ibid.*, pp. 35-36.

[In the novels of customs one needs a wealth of fine observation and accuracy and for historical novels, knowledge and sound criteria are indispensable. Otherwise there will be produced only ridiculous monstrosities . . .]

[2]Moreno Cora: *La crítica literaria en México,* Orizaba, Ver., Mayo de 1907. Tip. Artes y Oficio Teodoro A. Dehesa, p. 54.

[Altamirano more than any other writer exercised great influence on the studious youth of his country.]

una influencia decisiva en la marcha de los acontecimientos.[1]

González Peña is not less enthusiastic in his
praise:

> Altamirano es el más grande escritor de su
> tiempo.[2]

> . . . realiza una de las más extraordinarias carreras
> que la historia de nuestras letras registra; es el
> maestro de dos generaciones; trabaja activamente
> en la prensa; da el tono en la crítica literaria;
> estimula y alienta a los que comienzan . . .[3]

An examination of his literary prose, poetry
and critical articles and a study of his activities
in originating and directing literary societies
composed of writers justify the statements
quoted. But as a critic Altamirano's kind, fa-
therly feeling led him to praise some young writ-

---

[1] Julio Jiménez Rueda: *Historia de la literatura
mexicana,* México, 1928, p. 185.

[Poet, novelist, teacher, in his time he had a decisive influence on the march of events.]

[2] Carlos González Peña: *op. cit.,* p. 381.

[Altamirano is the greatest writer of his time.]

[3] *Ibid.,* pp. 380-381.

[. . . he made for himself one of the most extraordinary careers that the history of our literature records; he is the teacher of two generations; he works
actively in the press; he gives guidance in literary
criticism; he stimulates and encourages those who
are beginning . . .]

ers to their hurt. His desire to encourage kept him from being as severe as his role demanded. In discussing Florencio del Castillo's work, for instance, he called the young writer:

> . . . un escritor distinguido que fué honra de las bellas letras mexicanas . . .[1]

Such empty phrase-making indicates that Altamirano was too prone to let his kindness soften his criticism.

ENRIQUE OLAVARRÍA Y FERRARI

Enrique Olavarría y Ferrari, born in 1844[2] of Spanish parents, came to Mexico in 1865. Iguíniz did not list his works in his bibliography, claiming that he was not a Mexican. Olavarría's own statement shows that he considered Mexico his home, his country by adoption,[3] with whose life he had identified himself

---

[1] I. M. Altamirano: *Florencio del Castillo*, in *Renacimiento*, 1869, Vol. I, p. 500.

[. . . a distinguished writer who was the honor of Mexican belles lettres.]

[2] Carlos González Peña: *op. cit.*, p. 456.

[3] In a statement dated 1884, placed at the end of Series one, part one, p. iv of the collected episodes, second edition, the author wrote that he had been in Mexico nineteen years, that he became a naturalized Mexican, had married a Mexican, and that all his children were Mexicans.

completely, and whose institutions he studied as few native Mexicans had studied them. The fact that practically all his voluminous work is concerned with Mexican history, with Mexican scenes and people, with careful study of the development of Mexican institutions makes his exclusion unwarranted. If one refuses to consider him a Mexican, because he was not born in Mexico, he must for the same reason take George Santayana from America, Alarcón from Spain, José María de Heredia and Leconte de Lisle from France, though of course, when Olavarría came to Mexico he was older than those writers were when they entered their respective adopted countries. But expansion of this discussion would be more academic than practical.

Olavarría's work occupies a unique place in Mexican fiction in that he began the attempt to do for the historical novel in Mexico what Pérez Galdós did in Spain with his *Episodios nacionales,* though with much less literary merit.

This author's first two novels, *El tálamo y la horca,* and *Venganza y remordimiento* were published in 1868 and 1869 respectively. In 1880 he began the publication of a series of what he called *Episodios nacionales mexicanos* dealing with outstanding episodes of the history of Mexico and patterned after the first episodes of Galdós' series.

Of himself he wrote that his aim was to arrive at the exact historical truth,[1] and to present that truth in a form attractive to those who have little liking for the dryness of a formal historical treatise;[2] but he attacked the tendency of some historical novelists to permit an excess of imagination to interfere with accuracy.[3] He made no claim to literary excellence, or broad knowledge of the world's literature, and stated that he did not even possess the encyclopedias that many writers quoted to show their erudition;[4] but he contended that he brought to the historical novel the impartiality, good faith,[5] and careful study of history necessary for accuracy. Of the partisan attitude evident in much Mexican literature of historical nature he said:

. . . y tan no soy de este siglo . . . que me callo por no decir disparates con tono dogmático, ciencia

---

[1] Enrique Olavarría y Ferrari: *Episodios históricos mexicanos*, Series II, part one, p. 29.

[2] *Ibid.*, end of Series I, part one, p. vi.

[3] *Ibid.*, Series II, part one, p. 29.

[4] *Ibid.*

[5] *Ibid.*, end of Series I, part one, p. vi.

llevada al presente a un grado increíble de per-
fección . . . No sé tampoco criticar a los demás
con ese encarnizamiento que demuestra en el crítico
el deseo de reinar, como tuerto que es, en tierra de
ciegos.[1]

Olavarría complained of the lack of care in
the preservation of documents of Mexican history, and of the fact that many of those that were
preserved were too full of political passion to
be of value.[2]

His collection of episodes is divided into two
series of two parts each as follows:

First series, part one: *Las perlas de la reina
Luisa* (1808), *La Virgen de Guadalupe* (1809-
1810), *La derrota de las Cruces* (1810), *La
Virgen de los Remedios* (1810), *El puente de
Calderón* (1810-1811), *Las norias de Baján*,
(1811), *El treinta de julio* (1811), *El cura de
Nucupétaro* (1811), *La junta de Aitacuaro*
(1811-1812).Part two: *El sitio de Cuautla*

---

[1]*Ibid.*, Series II, part one, pp. 29-30.

[. . . and I am so alien to this century . . . that I keep
silence lest I say foolish things in dogmatic tone, an
art carried at present to an incredible degree of
perfection . . . Neither do I know how to criticise
others with that cruelty that reveals in the critic
the will to govern, like the one-eyed fellow that
he is, in a kingdom of blind men.]
[2]*Ibid.*, end of Series I, part one, p. v.

(1812), *Una venganza insurgente* (1812), *La constitución del año doce* (1812-1813), *El castillo de Acapulco* (1813), *El 22 de diciembre de 1815* (1813-1815), *El Conde de Venadito* (1816-1820), *Las tres garantías* (1820-1821), *La independencia* (1821), *El cadalso de Padilla* (1821-1824).

Second series, part one: *Carne de horca* (1823-1824), *Los coyotes* (1824), *San Juan de Ulúa* (1825), *Las gallinas* (1826-1827), *El motín de la Acordada* (1828), *La expedición de Burradas* (1829), *Los hombres de bien* (1829-1830), *La traición de Picaluga* (1831), *El plan de Zavaleta* (1831-1832). Part two: *El treinta y tres* (1833), *El gobierno de Herodes* (1833), *La estrella de los magos* (1834), *La tela de Penélope* (1834), *A las puertas del cielo* (1834), *La aurora del centralismo* (1835), *El comandante Paraja* (1836), *La vuelta de Tejas* (1836), *Justicia de Dios* (1836-1838).[1]

There is a lack of uniformity of merit in this long series of episodes. Some of them are interesting as fiction, as history and as *costum-*

---

[1] The dates in parentheses after these items are the dates of the respective events on which the stories are based.

brista prose; on the other hand, some of them have nothing to recommend them as fiction. The justice of the exclusion of some of them from consideration as literature must be clear in view of the fact that they are mere compilations of quotations of historical documents. *El treinta y tres*, out of 131 pages, has 99 quoted, *El gobierno de Herodes* contains 85 pages of quotations out of a total of 97. The episodes that, like these, are mere copies of source material are definitely not worth classifying as fiction.

But there are some that must be reckoned with in an extensive study of the Mexican historical novel, and a few are quite interesting in the arrangement of material, in the clear and imaginative interpretation of facts and forces, and in the understanding they give of Mexican psychology.

La constitución del año doce, Series 1, part two, pages 1225-1351, has as its central narrative the romantic love affair of Fernández de Lizardi and a beautiful girl named Remedios, with Anastasio de Ochoa playing a constant but insignificant role as the friend of the engaged couple and adviser of "El Pensador." García

Alonso, a wealthy rake of noble family stole Remedios and lived with her for some time without marrying her. The young lady forgot Fernández de Lizardi and fell in love with her captor who soon died leaving his fortune to her.

Remedios' spiritual advisers attempted to persuade her to take the veil and to leave her property to the church; her refusal to do so made her the victim of obstinate persecution at the hands of the interested parties. Later Álvaro de Cervera and his henchman, Centelles, initiated a scheme to get Remedios to marry the former in order to get her money; but it developed that she was the illegitimate daughter of her intended husband. The crafty schemer, Centelles, was then revealed as Captain Francisco Mejía.

Because this episode contains comparatively few strictly historical details and has relatively more sustained consideration of the demands of fiction for freedom and imagination, it is less like formal history than some of the others, and more like a historical novel from which objective minutiae have been sifted. The love affair hinges on the usual hero, the stricken maiden and villain.

This episode recites in considerable detail a

part of the struggle in the *Cortes de Cádiz* lead-
ing up to the establishment of the Constitution
of 1812. The recital is in the form of an un-
signed letter which the author reputedly found
and which he attributed to Lucas Alamán. It
covers nearly six large pages of close print.

There follows much interesting material on
the newspapers of the day, including, among
many others, *El Pensador Mexicano* of Fernández de Lizardi and *El Juguetillo* of Carlos Bustamante. The rambling comments on the press
are interesting, though too direct and prominent for proper balance in a novel.

Concerning the collection of the material for
this episode the author wrote:

> Formadas están estas páginas con lo que *tirios* y
> *troyanos* han dicho en papeles y libros que, con un
> afán superior a lo fatigoso de la tarea, he buscado y
> leído, dejando a cada uno de los elementos que
> forman el mosaico de mi obra, su lugar propio,
> bueno o malo, justo o injusto . . .[1]

The principal attraction of the work is the

---

[1]*Ibid.*, Series I, part two, p. 1226.

[These pages are made up of what *Tyrians* and
Trojans have written in manuscripts and in books
which, with a zeal superior to the tedium of the
task, I have sought and read, leaving to each one
of the items that make up the mosaic of my work
its proper place, good or bad, just or unjust.]

author's synthesis of the forces at work in Mexican society, his evaluation and interpretation of the causes of the revolution and the state of affairs of 1812. It becomes clear that the colonial regime had to fall of its own weight, that the people were not capable of removing the debris, and that nobody in Mexico had a definite, adequate plan for the future. His picture of complete impotence is quite effective, though rather didactic and direct for literary purposes.

El castillo de Acapulco continues the story of Mexican affairs, beginning where *La constitución del año doce* left off; i. e., with the recall of Venegas and the appointment of Calleja as viceroy. The author included in the first thirty-five pages a rather animated narration of an affair between Calleja and the actress Inés García and of the celebrations in Calleja's honor. Considerable space is given to a reproduction of conversations at a social function. With chapter VIII, p. 1389, there begins the usual faithful relation of historical events attested to by documents which the author cites in the manner of formal historians.[1] This lat-

---

[1] For example see *ibid.*, pp. 1395-1397.

ter part lacks artistic merit principally because
of the author's desire for historical accuracy.

He wove into this episode, as indeed he did
in practically all the others, many historical
characters and happenings without considering
their relation to the central plot; for example,
the story of the love of Andrés Quintana Róo
for Leona Vicario and their subsequent marriage. The work comes near to being a jumble
of interesting episodes and side lights gleaned
from various sources, true in substance, but having little to do with the central theme, interpolated with complete disregard for the demands
of coherence and unity. Olavarría seemingly
could not pass silently by any interesting incident in the life of a historical character,
whether that incident was germane to the general
movement of affairs or not. An example of the
inclusion of extraneous material is the threatened imprisonment of the wife of Bustamante.[1]
The author was evidently aware of this weakness, for he tried to justify it by saying that he
ought not to

[1]See pages 1414-1417.

. . . echar en olvido suceso alguno merecedor de
pasar al conocimiento de mis lectores.[1]

This statement reveals a lack of understanding
of the nature of true historical fiction.

The first episode of the second series is
Carne de horca, memorias de un criollo, 1823-
1824.It depicts the great enthusiasm of the Mexican people over their newly won independence,
and their equally great incapacity to govern
themselves. The lengthy discussion of political
developments in France and in Spain during
the first part of the nineteenth century is interesting, but occupies more space than is fitting.
The aim was to show the force of world movement toward liberalism and its effect on Mexico. From Chapter III to the end, this episode
is little more than a commented chronicle dealing with political events and the personnel of
the government after Iturbide's abdication, and
the troubles of the young republic, the greatest of
which was the struggle between the centralists
and the federalists. The author placed considerable emphasis on what he called "el cuadro

[1]*Ibid.,* p. 1421.
[. . . forget any happening whatsoever that is
worthy of being told to my readers.]

en que han de desarrollarse los acontecimientos."[1]

As in many of his other stories, Olavarría
included rather lengthy criticism of the literature of the period. Practically all of chapter IV
deals with the literature of the third decade of
the nineteenth century, especially with the
drama and with journalism. The author followed here the example of Mariano José de
Larra.

Of conditions in general he had much to say.
Politics he pictured as absorbing the interest of
all classes as a new game might have done.
Writers without judgment contributed their
talents to the creation of chaos, and visionary
patriots vied with predatory groups for control
of the government. His summary is interesting:

> Contábamos apenas dos años de haber consumado
> nuestra independencia y ya salíamos a dos pro-
> nunciamientos por mes: hubiese parecido aquello
> juego de chiquillos a no ser por los funestos re-
> sultados.[2]

---

[1]*Ibid.*, Series II, part one, pp. 29.
["the background in which events are to unfold."]
[2]*Ibid.*, p. 83.

[Scarcely two years had passed since we gained
our independence, and we were bringing out two
pronunciamientos a month; it would have seemed

The fictional part of *Carne de horca* is a mystery story, involving the hatred of the federalists for the Spaniards. Anievas and his lover Amparo were accused of attempting to strangle and to poison Francisco, the brother of Amparo; but it developed that their political enemies were the criminals guilty of a plot to kill all members of the Spanish family.

Whatever merit is assigned to *Carne de horca* must be on the ground of its historical accuracy in the descriptions of the period, for it is poor as fiction.

Los coyotes gets its name from the fact that Spaniards were called *coyotes* by the liberals.[1] It is a continuation of the preceding episode and has the same general tone and procedure. Even the secret plotting is continued, this time as an activity of a secret gang of terrorists. The Spaniards are pictured as victims of fanatic attempts against their property and lives, insulted in the press, and treated unjustly in the courts.

---

a childish game if the results had not been so deplorable.]

[1] The conservative creoles were called *acoyotados* and *borbonistas*.

Olavarría began *San Juan de Ulúa* with a discussion of newspapers in 1825, saying:

> Todo el mundo habíase improvisado literato y escritor . . . para ser periodista bastaba tener la voluntad de serlo.[1]

In a tone reminiscent of Mariano José de Larra the author has Fernández de Lizardi give his views on the state of journalism. An inside view of a newspaper office is included. One of the characters is made to predict that habits formed during the fight for independence and encouraged by official catering to attacks on Spaniards would develop a race of bandits in Mexico. Another expressed ideas that quite evidently were those of the author concerning the motives for hatred of the Spaniards who remained in the country:

> . . . no es el patriotismo el que os mueve a aborrecer a los españoles, sino la envidia que os causan sus riquezas y el deseo que tenéis de apoderaros de ellas y disfrutarlas vosotros que no las habéis adquirido iguales porque no sabéis trabajar ni habéis nacido para ello.[2]

---

[1] [Everybody had suddenly become a literary man and a writer . . . to be a journalist all that was needful was the will to be one.]

[2] Enrique Olavarría y Ferrari: *San Juan de Ulúa,* p. 198.

[. . . it is not patriotism that moves you to hate

The first three chapters contain a critical summary of the conditions existing in Mexico, most of which is given in the conversation of two political sophists. In his comments on literature of the day Olavarría remarked that Lizardi had been unable to sell enough of the second edition of *Periquillo* to pay the cost of printing; that the only kind of writing the people were interested in was cheap doggerel verse composed by courageous ignoramuses. One character facetiously stated that he learned much of it by heart in order to have a better opinion of his own compositions. Olavarría's attack on such false poetry is severe, bitingly severe,[1] and his remarks on the theatre are little less so.[2] Of Mexican music he had a better opinion.[3] He gives a brief view of such matters as popular celebrations, dances and other diversions, the state of education, lawlessness,[4] lack of sani-

the Spaniards, but the envy that their wealth arouses in you, the desire you have to get your hands on that wealth and enjoy it, you who have not acquired as much because you do not know how to work nor were you born for work.]

[1]*Ibid.*, pp. 218-219 and p. 224.
[2]*Ibid.*, p. 227.
[3]*Ibid.*
[4]*Ibid.*, p. 231.

tation, epidemics,[1] conflicts between the York masons and Scottish masons,[2] gleaned from every available source.

The sources of information used by Olavarría include the better known collections of historical material; and though most of those sources are fragmentary, he attempted by comparison to balance those of liberal leanings against those of conservative bent. For instance, Bustamente and Alamán were used for reciprocal correction. It is not possible to include in the limits of this work a detailed study of the sources of all his episodes, but a few will give a satisfactory understanding of the author's procedure.

In *El sitio de Cuautla* the general character of each of the insurgent leaders is essentially the same as that painted by Juan A. Mateos in his novel dealing with the same siege. Many of the interesting details are historical in substance, v. gr., Morelos' sally with a small guard, his rescue by Galeana, and Fernández' heroism in saving the life of Galeana agree with the account contained in Ward's *Mexico in 1827*[3]

---

[1]*Ibid.*, pp. 230-231.

[2]*Ibid.*, p. 244.

[3]Published in 1828. See Vol. I, pp. 190-191.

and in Bancroft's *History of Mexico*.[1] This episode, for all of its historicity, ceases to be formal history in Olavarría's hands. He succeeds in making the characters re-enact their historical roles before the gaze of the reader, not as political leaders, but as men of flesh and blood. The epic note is prominent in the description of personal courage. Venegas' encouragement at the arrival of two Spanish batallions at Vera Cruz on January 14 and 16,[2] his stiffened attitude toward Calleja thereafter, his acceptance of the latter's resignation, the resulting resentment of the army and the final retraction of the viceregal acceptance of the resignation were taken from documented sources and used as a framework for the author's story.[3] Calleja's letter to Venegas, dated February 1, is quoted by Olavarría,[4] probably from Alamán's *Historia de México*.[5]

---

[1]Vol. IV, p. 363 and footnote 52 on same page.

[2]*Gaceta de México,* 1812, III, p. 114. See also Lucas Alamán: *Historia de México,* Vol. II, p. 469.

[3]Compare Bancroft: *op. cit.,* Vol. IV, p. 357. Also Alamán: *op. cit.,* Vol. II, pp. 472-473.

[4]Enrique Olavarría y Ferrari: *op. cit.,* Series I, part two, pp. 997-998.

[5]Lucas Alamán: *op. cit.,* Vol. II, pp. 473-475.

The author's description of the processional on the day of *San Felipe de Jesús* and of the celebration of Calleja's entrance into Mexico are in substance the same as Bancroft's later descriptions. The account of the military salutes and religious festivals given by Olavarría in Series I, part 2, page 1003 *et seq.* was taken from the *Gaceta de México*, 1812, III, pages 133-134, and from Alamán: *Historia de México*, II, pages 475-477. In Series I, part 2, page 1004, the author recorded the number of Calleja's men as it is recorded in Bustamante: *Campañas de Calleja*, page 167. In *El sitio de Cuautla*, pages 1018-1020, he included the substance of Venegas' report on conditions in Mexico City which he took from Bustamente: *ut sup.*, pages 159-165. Olavarría: *ut sup.*, page 1020, parallels Bustamante: *ut sup.*, pages 161 *et seq.*, in the plan of attack on Morelos as outlined by Venegas. Bustamante: *ut sup.*, pages 163-164, was the source of Olavarría's description of the march of Calleja as presented on page 1020 of *El sitio de Cuautla*, the two mentioning the same towns in the line of march and assigning the same reasons for the choice of the route.

Even the chronology of events as given by

Olavarría is rigidly historical. His general and scattered pictures of the brutality of both royalists and insurgents are in essential agreement with Bancroft's account found in Bancroft: *op. cit.*, Vol. IV, page 355, which was taken from Ward: *op. cit.*, Vol. I, page 189 and from Bustamante: *Cuadros históricos*, Vol. I, page 323. Olavarría's remark on the silence of the *Gaceta de México* on Calleja's defeat, found in Olavarría: *ut sup.*, page 1027, reveals the fact that he had studied its columns. The report of the failure of the attack on Cuautla and the statement of necessity for a siege sent by Calleja to Venegas, contained in Olavarría: *ut sup.*, pages 1028-1031, came from Bustamante's *Campañas de Calleja*, pages 170-171.

Olavarría, in *ut sup.*, page 1036, quoted Calleja's letter dated March 13 dealing with the heroic resistance of the insurgents; this letter is found also in Bustamante: *Cuadros históricos*, Vol. II, page 58. He made a truly literary episode out of the story of Francisco Ayala which he found in Bustamante: *ut sup.*, Vol. II, pages 35-37. Bancroft in *op. cit.*, Vol. IV, page 363 stated in a footnote that Alamán, in his *Historia de México*, Vol. II, page 428, verified Bustamante's account on the authority of reliable persons in Cuautla. The account of the death of Gil Riaño found in Olavarría: *ut sup.*, page 1063, was taken with slight additions from Alamán's *Historia de México*, Vol. II, page 515. Olavarría's contention that Calleja considered the siege hopeless and begged Venegas to give it up is supported by Negrete: *México en el siglo xix*, Vol. IV, pages 438-439.

In *Una venganza insurgente*, Series I, part 2, Olavarría continued to follow the accounts of Bustamante, Negrete, Alamán and various individual reports, some of which were published in the *Gaceta de México*. The flight of Col. Manuel Sosa, Leonardo Bravo and José Mariana de la Piedra from Cuautla and their subsequent capture at the hacienda of San Gabriel, an estate belonging to Gabriel Yermo, as related in *Una Venganza insurgente*, pages 1096-1098 is accurate in substance. The same incident is cited in the *Gaceta de México*, 1812, III, 488, 722-724, Negrete: *op. cit.*, Vol. V, page 13, and Bustamante: *Cuadros históricos*, Vol. II, page 73.

Some idea of Olavarría's tendency to paraphrase in his narration the material he found in histories and chronicles may be had from a comparison of the following versions:

> Bravo and Sosa attempted to defend themselves; the former was thrown down and bound and the latter killed on the spot. Piedra quietly surrendered.[1]

> (Sosa) . . . se arrojó sobre los asaltanes, y éstos hicieron fuego sobre él y le tendieron muerto a sus pies.

> D. Leonardo quiso también defenderse, pero uno de aquellos temibles campesinos se lanzó sobre él, y tomándole de los brazos por la espalda, le arrojó en tierra, y allí otros muchos le amarraron . . . Piedras se entregó sin resistencia . . .[2]

It is quite evident that Bancroft and Olavarría used the same sources; Bancroft's are given as *Gaceta de México,* 1812, III, pages 488, 722-724; Negrete: *op. cit.,* Vol. V, page 13, and Bustamante: *Cuadros históricos,* II, page 73.

The story of the capture, the trial and the

---

[1]Bancroft: *op. cit.,* Vol. IV, p. 409. Bancroft too was merely paraphrasing his sources.

[2]Enrique Olavarría y Ferrari: *ut sup.,* p. 1098.

[(Sosa) . . . threw himself on the assailants, and the latter fired on him and killed him at their feet.

D. Leonardo also tried to defend himself, but one of those terrible farmers leaped on him and taking him by the arms behind his back, threw him to the ground, and there many others bound him . . . Piedras surrendered without resistance.]

execution of José Antonio Torres as given by Olavarría in *ut sup.*, pages 1101-1102, is essentially the same as that found in Negrete: *op. cit.*, V, pages 57-64, in Bustamante: *Cuadros históricos*, I, page 145, Zerecero: *Memorias para la historia de las revoluciones mexicanas*, 1869, pages 182-188, Alamán: *ut sup.*, III, pages 184-186, and in Mora: *México y sus revoluciones*, IV, pages 439-442.

In this episode Olavarría y Ferrari followed very closely the outline of his historical sources. There is a wealth of minor incidents, most of which are historical; v. gr., the celebration that took place as Torres was paraded through the streets.[1]

That Olavarría knew well Negrete's attitude is indicated by the fact that in *ut sup.*, page 1100, he charges Negrete with being a hater of the insurgents, saying that his discourse is full of such epithets as "miserable bandits, cowardly assassins, infamous rebels." Incidentally on page 387 of *History of Mexico*, Vol. IV, including the footnote, Bancroft wrote that Negrete

Never spoke of the insurgents without using

---

[1]*Ibid.*, pp. 1101 to 1102, and Bancroft: *op. cit.*, Vol. IV, pp. 388-389.

some blackening epithet . . . Monsters, infamous rebels, wretches, cowardly assassins, vile canaille and such like . . .

Olavarría in *ut sup.*, pages 1104-1106 quoted from Bustamante nearly two pages of material on the bandit leaders who associated themselves with the insurgents.

The author's acquaintance with periodical literature of the epoch treated is shown in such comments as those found in *ut sup.*, pages 1126-1127.

A comparison of Olavarría's treatment of the events surroundings the death of Leonardo Bravo and of the unique vengeance taken by his son Nicolás Bravo with accounts found in Bustamante, *Cuadros históricos*, II, pages 161-162, Alamán, *Historia de México*, III, pages 259-261, Negrete, *México en el siglo xix*, *V*, pages 191-195, 312-313, and Tornel y Mendívil, *Resumen histórico*, pages 140-141 will leave no uncertainty as to Olavarría's sources in this instance.

In several of his episodes Olavarría used material from Zavala's history; for example, *San Juan de Ulúa*, pages 270-271, *Las Gallinas*, page 316, and chapters viii, ix, and x. Chapter ii of *El motín de la Acordada* begins with

material taken mostly from Tornel y Mendívil's
Reseña histórica.

At the time of their publication Olavarría's
episodes were the most complete commentaries
on Mexican history in the form of fiction. Nothing escaped the author's attention. His work is
a critical summary of practically all forces,
conditions, and attitudes, and of literature and
art.

His work abounds in such unerring analyses
as that of the lower class found in *El motín de
la Acordada,* in which he paints the depravity of
the free peons and their mentors just as faithfully as he had painted in previous episodes the
heroism of oppressed peons and their leaders
when they were fighting for liberty. As oppressed people inspired by the ideals of liberty
they were deserving of pity and honor; as free
men they were ignorant, depraved, licentious
bandits, robbing, plundering, beastly monsters.
When those who fought for justice became the
enemies of justice, Olavarría followed faithfully the record, even though such a procedure
in many instances destroyed the force of his
work as fiction. Though he was sympathetic to
the aspirations of a people fighting for its right

to live as it chose, he sternly rebuked the abuses of that people and its inability to govern itself once it was free, sometimes using original invective and sometimes quoting such opinions as the following of Zavala:

> La cosa más insignificante, los negocios personales se hacían materia de discusiones públicas, objetos de combate entre las facciones políticas; una y otra obraban con imprudencia, sin miramientos, por puro deseo de sobreponerse.[1]

Olavarría in several instances boldly attacked literary critics for giving Mexican literature a value it did not have, charging that in all the colonial period Mexico had only two writers worth mentioning, Sor Juana Inés de la Cruz and Alarcón. He charged in *La estrella de los magos* that the literary activities of the early days of independence were mostly those of pamphleteers and professional libelists. In *El sitio de Cuautla*, part of Series I, part two, chapters v and vi, the author presented various samples of doggerel verse characteristic of the

---

[1]Olavarría y Ferrari: *San Juan de Ulúa*, p. 270.

[The most insignificant thing, personal affairs became matters of public debate, objects of combat between political factions; all factions conducted themselves without prudence, without circumspection, for the sheer desire to rule.]

period. He discussed the society of poets called *Arcadia Mexicana* whose president was called *mayoral* and whose members were called *zagales*. He reviewed their work published in *El diario de México* under such pseudonyms as *Flagastro Cieve, Batilo, Aminto, Cioslapa, Tirsis, Damón, Ascanio, el Aplicado, Anfriso, Noatino Glosado, Antimio, etc.* These formal reviews and many others scattered through several of the episodes, while not fitting in a novelistic work, add to the value of the work as criticism of the period. It will be seen later that Salado Álvarez followed this tendency in his work.

The reader has probably already come to the conclusion that the work of Olavarría is a selection and arrangement of historical and critical materials, with a few amenities added for interest; and that the only elements of fiction are found in the detailed dialogues and actions of historical personages, all of which are kept in close subjection to historical facts in general. But even so, Olavarría rose occasionally to the level of true fiction. In scattered episodes his characters slipped out of the narrow historical frame and became individuals of great interest in their own right. Many intimate glimpses of their souls in travail, accepting nobly their lot with determined loyalty to principle, add a sense of inspired beauty that always accompanies human greatness. But that atmosphere does not pervade the entire episode. Olavarría's weakness is not that he never reached the level of pure art, but that he could not consistently maintain that level. The truly fictional characters are few, and at times the parade of historical personages is bewildering. One not interested in the mass of details and in the personnel of the conflicts will find his patience taxed.

The style is uneven, being an alternation, not a mixture, of the novelistic and the formally historical. There is little empty ornate language, the bombastic style common in that day in Mexico being agreeably lacking; indeed the sentences are so plain, simple and unconnotative that the style is at times bare.

F. Gómez Flores esteemed the historical narratives of Olavarría because they furnished a reliable source of information in a form that the Mexican public, little addicted to serious unadorned history, could read with interest.[1] He

---

[1]*Mazatlán literaria,* Mazatlán, 1889, pp. 36-37.

supported Olavarría's contention that Mexican critics assigned literary value to a host of writings that had none.[1] The director of *La Voz de Mazatlán* remarked that Olavarría's procedure was so clear that the reader never confused the fictional with the historical.[2] This statement, though meant as praise, is in reality an indictment of Olavarría on his greatest weakness. His failure to let his historical materials fuse with his fictional material into a truly unified literary presentation of history is by all odds his major deficiency.

The work is not a recreation like Scott's *Ivanhoe*, nor is it so heavily charged with fancy and fictitious elements as the works of Dumas. In purpose, it is more like the writings of Erkmann-Chatrian and Pérez Galdós, though quite inferior to those of the latter in plan, balance, style and originality of treatment. There is frequently an attempt at drama through sublimation of the characters.

Olavarría's work is poor fiction. His basic error was the result of a lack of understanding of the nature of literature in general and of fic-

[1] *Ibid.*, p. 37.
[2] *Ibid.*

tion in particular. This lack of orientation resulted in confusion of the aims of art and those of history. In his inability to create fiction he turned to the devices of the critic and historian.

One may ask, then, why this rather extensive treatment of him. It must be kept in mind that this study proposes to show the development of the historical novel; and Olavarría y Ferrari is one of the stages of that development. Furthermore, the weaknesses revealed in his procedure were present in much of Mexican historical fiction until the end of the period with which we are concerned. No other single factor contributed so much to the sterility of Mexican historical novelists as the misconceptions of the basic nature of fiction and the relation of history thereto. The fact that in many cases historical accuracy was the goal sought made impossible the development of fiction comparable to that of European nations.

VICENTE RIVA PALACIO

Vicente Riva Palacio was born in Mexico City in 1832. His chief interests were law, literature and politics. During his lifetime he was a brigadier-general in the fight against French intervention, Minister of Public Welfare, Governor of Michoacán and of the state of Mexico, a judge of the Supreme Court of Mexico, and an envoy extraordinary and minister plenipotentiary to Madrid. But whatever his position, he always wrote, some times in political newspapers of his own founding, like *El azote,* some times as co-editor of compilations and more or less formal works, such as *El libro rojo* and *México a través de los siglos.* His original work consists of various kinds of poetry and prose.

Riva Palacio's first historical novel, *Calvario y Tabor,* was published in 1868. There were five editions in all, in the years 1868, 1883, 1905, 1908, and 1923 respectively. The first edition has 589 pages and contains a prologue by Ignacio Manuel Altamirano.

This novel begins with a description of the physical aspects of nature and of the inhabitants of San Luis on the Pacific coast. The narrative is begun by the relation of a trick played on a man while he was drunk. The man, made to believe that he had killed the mayor while under the influence of alcohol, fled the country never to return, abandoning his family without any explanation whatever. The wife left in search of him, leaving the little daughter in the care of the friend who had arranged the joke.

The fugitive quite accidentally found his daughter, Alejandra, after she was grown. He then related the story of his experiences.

The tale is full of abrupt changes. The style is choppy in many places, paragraphs of one short sentence following each other monotonously. There are violence and sensational episodes almost without end; for instance, one character's hand was hacked off because a snake bit him, a girl was abducted and her escort shot, a whole army was intrigued into eating poisonous fruit by an imperialist spy, and the imperialists killed the sick victims who either had not died or had not crawled off. Even a rabid dog adds sensation. There are secrets, orphans, subversive plots, rivalries, battles, monsters of iniquity, and brave soldiers of angelic character. The whole work is a miscellany of love affairs and military episodes. There is no balance and little regard for unity of action in the plot.

Riva Palacio's second novel was *Monja y casada, virgen y mártir* of which *Martín Garatuza* is a sequel. The first had four editions: the first in 1868, one in 1900, one in 1908, and another without date; *Martín Garatuza* also had four editions: the first in 1868, two in 1908, and the other undated.

The characters of these two novels were all still born, for not one of them is a live human; and the historical background is so unconvincingly presented as to be of little value. The women are either perfect in goodness and beauty and usually the victims of villainous plots, or are entirely evil; and the heroes are wholly admirable and the villains are incredibly depraved. But none of the goodness, beauty, nobility or depravity is convincing; otherwise, effectiveness might have resulted. Riva Palacio in these two novels leaves the impression of superficiality of emotion as one who knew the mechanical tricks of plot, but had not the ability to create character. He insists on telling directly or indirectly that his characters are what he wants them to be instead of creating with the artist's touch the beauty and nobility or depravity he wants to portray. This work is sterile as far as artistic creation is concerned.

The style is heavily serious throughout; no light wit or irony or satirical passage is to be found. Variety of tone does not exist.

In short, the weaknesses of these two novels are practically the same as those of *Calvario y Tabor;* and in our opinion they are sufficient to justify the termination of this criticism without further comment.

Las dos empedradas, published first in 1869, again in 1908, and a third time in 1909, begins with a discussion of a division in the court of Mariana of Austria after the death of Phillip IV. It presents the rivalry between Nitardo, the Jesuit confessor of the Queen, and Juan de Austria, the illegitimate son of Phillip IV. The characters are then transferred to Mexico. The remainder of the story is a ceaseless round of intrigues, jealousies, crimes and vengeance, in which the author exhausts his imagination for the sake of sensations he never quite arouses.

Los piratas del golfo, published first in 1869 and again in 1908, merits more study than the preceding novels. Brazo de Acero, a hunter of wild cattle in the island of Española was the lover of a girl named Julia. Pedro de Borica, a typical villain, waylaid Julia one night when she was returning from a tryst with Brazo de Acero and tried to attack her. The great Juan Morgan, most noted of the pirates of his day, knowing beforehand the plans of Pedro, stepped from the bushes and sent the assailant fleeing. But Pedro finally married Julia's mother in order to be in a better position to carry out his designs on the girl.

Brazo de Acero met Morgan, admired him, and decided to become a member of his band. In a conversation between the two Morgan gave expression to some noble ideals that become the moving force of the chief characters. At this point the author succeeded in giving artistic form to his creation. Juan Morgan is made interesting and sufficiently strong to lead the reader to identify with him his own ideals of justice and right. Morgan's aim was to free the Americas of the tyranny of European rule; and he justified his crimes by contending that the end justified the means. When he captured a town he always retired to a secluded room in order not to see the excesses of his men, whom he knew he could not restrain.

Pedro, Julia, and her mother set out for Santo Domingo accompanied by the Spanish fleet. As a part of Morgan's plan to capture the entire fleet, Brazo de Acero took passage on one of the Spanish men-of-war in order to get information Morgan wanted. When the attack occurred he saved Julia from his fellow pirates by claiming that she was his wife. Julia and her family went on to Mexico, leaving Brazo de Acero with the pirates. The volume ends with the mystery of Brazo de Acero's identity unsolved.

The second part of the novel goes back several years beyond the time of the beginning of the first part, and takes up the story of a young count, Enrique Torreleal. This gallant, the most popular of the young set of his day, aroused the envy of a rival, Don Diego de Álvarez, by his successes in amorous adventures to such a degree that the latter set about to have him banished from Mexico. In his designs Don Diego was aided by Don Justo, brother of Enrique's stepmother, who would inherit the latter's husband's fortune if his son, Enrique, were out of the way. The youth was banished on a false charge of having abducted a girl named Ana with whom he had been in love; he went to Española, where he became known as Brazo de Acero, hunter of wild cattle.

During a pirate attack on Portobello Enrique saved Diego's life and his wife's honor from the pirates. Diego, grateful for Enrique's service, revealed the fact that the latter had been exiled on false charges, and secured his pardon. In the meantime, Enrique's father had died, leaving a will in which he specified that if his son did not appear by a certain date, his fortune was to go to his second wife and her brother, Justo. Enrique appeared on the last day of grace and saved his fortune. His lover, Julia, had been forced to accept an arrangement of marriage to Justo; but the wedding ceremony was stopped before the final vows were taken, and Enrique married her.

This brief resumé will be sufficient to reveal the essential nature of the plot. The weaknesses are many: lack of natural development of plot; an excess of sub-plots; an abundance of ramifications and disconnected threads that are forced to merge into one grand finale; lack of sustained character portrayal, and unmotivated action.

La vuelta de los muertos is a story of Tetzahuitl, an Aztec prince, and his Aztec lover, Doña Isabel, who had been given a Christian name and married to a Spaniard. It is not of importance.

Memorias de un impostor is a story of the seventeenth century in Mexico. It is full of violence, incredible episodes, murder and abuses of the Inquisition without unity of purpose.

JUAN A. MATEOS

This author was born in Mexico in 1831. As a student he came under the influence of Ignacio Ramírez, the fervent and implacable apostle of liberalism and teacher of a generation that sponsored the movement for reform. It was the influence of Ramírez that determined the social and political attitudes of Juan A. Mateos.

Like most ambitious young men of his day, Mateos studied law and became involved in politics. He entered the army during the revolution of Ayutla; he took up arms on the side of the liberals throughout the War of Reform, and again later in the fight against the French invasion. Reconciled at one time with the imperialists, he was made Alderman of Mexico City. An attack on Maximilian in the press was the cause of his arrest and imprisonment in San Juan de Ulúa; but he escaped and joined the forces of Juárez. When the Empire was overthrown he was made Secretary of the Supreme

Court of Mexico and later became a deputy to the National Congress.

Mateos' numerous contributions to the press and his public discourses were characterized by uncompromising loyalty to the liberal cause. Like Ramírez and Altamirano, he fought for the destruction of the old regime and the inauguration of a liberal program. Patriotic sentiment is the guiding force in all his interpretations.

The first novel of Juan A. Mateos was called *El Cerro de las Campanas*. The first edition, on which no date appears, was published in Mexico in 1868 and the second in Buenos Aires. It has little stylistic attraction; its language is monotonous and consistently inflated with empty rhetoric, and the reader is annoyed with the arbitrary and accidental nature of its transitions. The style is at times choppy; for example, the first ten paragraphs are of one sentence each, averaging two lines each in length. This jolting movement at times is made to flatten into monotonous strides without variety.

But the deficiencies of style are no greater than those of arrangement of material. So without order is it that the progression gives con-

stantly the impression of being forced, unnatural, hastily improvised, and loosely
thrown together. The story is a series of connected chronicles with a love story that at times
is lost in a mass of historical material and then
reappears to lessen the monotony of historical
narration. One set of characters is put in motion, advanced to a given point, and abandoned
while the author brings forward other sets, one
at a time. The round is then repeated.

But in spite of its evident weaknesses of style
and arrangement of material, *El Cerro de las
Campanas* has been the public's history of the
period of the French intervention. It presents
a panorama of events from May 31, 1863, to
the death of Maximilian, a panorama colored
by the author's desire to give expression to his
liberal convictions by simplifying and synthe-
sizing the basic principles out of which the
facts of history sprang.

In answer to the charge that Mateos was not
moderate in his descriptions it may be contended
that his interpretation is the result of the liberal
idealism that had become almost a religion to
him. He identified the liberal cause with good
and the conservative opponents of liberalism

with evil. The perfection of liberalism was quite
real to him. It was the basis of his interpretation
and was the source of his inspiration. There is
evidence of his knowledge of the details of the
long struggle for national advance and an understanding of the positions, attitudes and actions
of the contending groups. To him the reform
movement was not an isolated phenomenon but
an episode in the chronic clash of interests that
had been in opposition in Mexico since the conquest, and in human society since the world
began. In one group he saw the ideals of social
justice; in the other group, the desire for the
preservation of special privilege and domination by any and all means. The respective
philosophies of the two groups, rather than individuals, are the real hero and the real villain
of his work.

The novel contains some interesting carica-
tures, but no true types. The *afrancesados* who
fawned at the feed of the French invaders in the
hope of gaining social and political advantage
are represented by the ridiculous Mr. and Mrs.
Fajardo. They and their kind, wearing wigs and
stiff shirts, trying to speak French instead of
Spanish, are ludicrous. This couple went to the

extreme of trying to change their name to one that sounded like French, and of trying to force their daughter to favor and even marry the first French soldier who proposed marriage. The entire group reminds one of the Greek-loving women of Moliere's *Les Femmes Savantes*. This humorous note serves to add variety to a story that would otherwise have been monotonous.

In *El Cerro de las Campanas* Mateos took his traditional attitude toward ecclesiasticism. He was thoroughly convinced that the clergy was a group of traitors offering their farcical blessings to the recently arrived French troops because they had come to protect the ecclesiastics' property and prestige, totally unconcerned that that protection was bought with their country's independence.

The general tone of *El Cerro de las Campanas* is melodramatic. The heroes, possessed of all the finer emotions of the human soul, weep like adolescents over separation from loved ones, yet fight like the Cid in battle. One of them was

    . . . un hombre que ríe de un muerto y llora al ver
a un desgraciado.[1]

---

[1]Juan A. Mateos:*El Cerro de las Campanas*, Maucci Hnos., México, n. d., called *novísima edición*. p. 24.

    [. . . a man who laughs at a dead man and who

El sol de mayo was published in Mexico in 1868. An edition printed in Buenos Aires and another in Genoa bear no dates. The action of the novel starts in July, 1861, four months after the date of the last events recorded in *Memorias de un guerrillero* by the same author, and ends with Juárez' abandonment of the City of Mexico, May 31, 1863, the event with which *El Cerro de las Campanas* begins.

It is divided into four parts as follows: *La cabeza del Bautista, Una cruzada en el siglo diez y nueve, Por derecho de conquista,* and *El sitio de Zaragoza.* It abounds in such details as the trial of Payno by the National Congress, his eloquent defense, and the spirited attacks made on him by Ignacio Manuel Altamirano. The work contains an interesting presentation of the diplomatic trickery of France in the manipulation of affairs in order to make an opportunity to intervene in Mexico. Mateos quoted the French ambassador to the effect that the French, aided by Mexican conservatives, had paid the press of Europe to create sentiment against Mexico and in favor of intervention, and that France's ultimate goal was to use Mexico as a base of opera-

weeps on seeing an unfortunate one.]

tions for a subsequent attempt to destroy the United States. The author's attempt was to present the liberal regime as abstract right fighting against the forces of retrogression and oppression. His historical facts were merely the raw material out of which he tried to build a structure in accord with his own ideals. But he lacked the skill necessary for unified and well-proportioned construction.

The author was a better historian than novelist, for this work is little more than a popularized and commented history of the period. His principal sources were the correspondence of the French and English ambassadors, found in the public archives to which as librarian of the National Congress Mateos had access; information taken from the correspondence files of public men of the day; published *actas* and *pronunciamientos* of the contending factions, such as *Acta levantada en la ciudad de Oaxaca* of April 20, 1862; proclamations like those of Almonte and Laurenciez; histories of localities, such as *Ensayo sobre una historia de Orizaba,* by Arroniz; military histories and diaries, for example, *Breve reseña de los sucesos de Guadalajara y de las lomas de Calderón,* the *Diario de*

*las operaciones y movimientos del ejército fe-
deral hasta su entrada a la capital de la República,* by Pérez Gallardo, and his own personal
experiences and those of his friends.

The literary aspects of *El sol de mayo* are not
essentially different from those of *El Cerro de
las Campanas* which we have already discussed.

Sacerdote y caudillo was published first in
1869, and again in 1902, and a third edition
printed in Buenos Aires bears no date.   This
novel, to which Altamirano correctly assigned
considerably more value than to Mateos' previous ones,[1] begins with an air of genuine realism
the description of the Rector of the *Colegio de
San Nicolás*. Mateos displayed in this description considerable artistry in recreating the general atmosphere of the epoch involved.   The
books Hidalgo left unhidden in his bookcase
are not merely a part of the background, but
important indications of the material permitted
the scholar in 1795 in Mexico, and the books he
secreted and which he read behind locked doors
reveal the nature of Hidalgo's mental and spiritual sympathies. The evolution of his ideas is
described briefly but sufficiently well that every

---

[1]*El renacimiento,* Vol. 1, 1869, p. 90.

man who has passed from a state of conventional orthodoxy to a more rational point of view will recognize therein a part of his own experience.

Hidalgo's liberalism, his trouble with the Inquisition, his kindness to the Indians, his knowledge of their dialects and his attempts to help them improve their agricultural methods and standard of living made of him a high priest of righteousness and kindness. Into the attitudes of Hidalgo Mateos put all that progressive liberalism aspired to. He was the champion of a new order of things in Mexico, the real father of modern Mexican progressivism, a truly noble soul.

The Inquisition and those who used it for their own ends played the role of powerful obstruction. The fact that Hidalgo revolted against its seemingly absolute and unlimited power, and that he later came to defy even the temporal representative of Spain makes of him a dramatic character.

Mateos' summary of the fight for freedom led by Hidalgo may be expressed in the words used by one of the characters:

. . . la revolución es la tendencia de una idea a

sobreponerse sobre un régimen, a variar el modo de
ser de una sociedad, y esa idea es precisamente la de
Hidalgo . . .[1]

Concerning the role of the people in the social structure of the old regime he remarked
with evident sorrow over the lot of the masses:

En cuanto al pueblo, no formaba clase alguna
de la sociedad.[2]

In his mind the preponderance of influence of
the wealthy creoles, of the army and of the
church, each with its privileges and exemptions,
had made justice impossible. He pictured these
groups as living in idle luxury while the people
were denied the essentials of decent existence.
He charged the conservatives with unpatriotic
and anti-social obstruction of progress.   This
spirit was the same as that which Mateos contended in *El Cerro de las Campanas* was flagrant
enough to invite the invasion of Mexico by a
foreign foe.

---

[1]Juan A. Mateos: *Sacerdote y caudillo*, Maucci,
México and Buenos Aires, n. d., p. 309.

[. . . the revolution is the tendency of an idea to
become master over a regime, the tendency to
change the spirit of a society, and that idea is the
conception of Hidalgo.]

[2]*Ibid.*, p. 308.

[So far as the common people were concerned,
they held no place whatever in society.]

In this novel, as in nearly all the others of Mateos, the clergy is severely satirized. A priest harangued as follows:

¡Matar! ¡Descuartizar! ¡Aniquilar! . . . tal es vuestro deber como ovejas del Señor.[1]

Mateos' interpretation of the events with which he dealt was consistently that of the profoundly patriotic liberal. IIis liberalism approached the plane of religious conviction.

The sources of this novel include almost every available account of the events of the period. That the author used them liberally and some times without giving credit to others will be clear upon examination of the following quotations taken from Mateos and Olavarría respectively:

En un rincón del aposento había una porción considerable de barras de plata recogidas en la Alhóndiga y manchadas todavía con sangre, en otro, una cantidad de lanzas y arrimado a la pared y suspendido de una de éstas, el cuadro con la imagen de Guadalupe.[2]

---

[1]*Ibid.*, p. 326.

[Kill! Cut to pieces! Annihilate! Such is your duty as lambs of God.]

[2]Juan A. Mateos: *Sacerdote y caudillo,* Maucci, México and Buenos Aires, 1902, part four, Chap. LIV, p. 330.

[In one corner of the room there was a considerable quantity of bars of silver taken in the

> . . . había en un rincón una porción considerable de barras de plata recogidas a los asaltanes de la Alhóndiga y manchadas aún de sangre, en otro una buena cantidad de lanzas, y arrimado a la pared y suspendido de una de aquéllas, el cuadro con la imagen de la Virgen de Guadalupe.[1]

Olavarría y Ferrari gave credit to Lucas Alamán for his quotation, though without indicating its limits or the specific source; but Mateos did not even suggest that the language he was using was not his own.

There are two characters that are well done in the story, Hidalgo and Riaño. Both are perfect models of abstract principles, sublimations of the best traits of humanity.

Los insurgentes had three editions, one printed in Mexico in 1869, one in Mexico in

---

Alhóndiga and still stained with blood, in another, a quantity of lances and leaning against the wall and hanging from one of the lances, the picture with the image of Guadalupe.]

[1]Olavarría y Ferrari: *Episodios históricos mexicanos.* Series I, part one, p. 295.

. . . there was in one corner a considerable quantity of bars of silver taken from those who attacked the Alhóndiga and still stained with blood, in another a good quantity of lances, and leaning against the wall and suspended from one of the former (i. e., lances) the picture with the image of the Virgin of Guadalupe.

1902, and another in Buenos Aires with no date mentioned. It is a continuation of *Sacerdote y caudillo,* beginning with the death of Hidalgo, the event with which *Sacerdote y caudillo* closed.

A fantastic factor of considerable interest is injected early into the story. It involved three emeralds taken during the conquest from the necklace of Xicoténcatl, the leader of the Tlaxcaltecans, and given to his three sons. Each son was to pass the emerald on to his oldest son, and so on generation after generation. The generation that saw the emeralds united in the hands of one man would be the generation chosen to bring independence from the Spanish invaders, but the possessor would die in the struggle. The gems fell into the hands of the leader of the insurgents at the beginning of the fight for independence. This legend fitted well into the story, providing a refreshing bit of fancy.

Memorias de un guerrillero was published in 1897. Another edition published by Maucci Hnos., Mexico, bears no date.

The story begins with the flight of Santa Anna in 1855 and continues to the entrance of Juárez into Mexico City, January 11, 1861.

Like the historical novels Mateos published previously, it is a parade of historical personages and presents the same conflicts and the same forces as the others, though with changed personnel. There is evident in this work, however, a better and calmer understanding of the difficulties involved in the move to reform the social structure of the nation. The author saw that the ignorance, fanaticism and mental inertia of the people, and not the opposition of the conservatives, was the greatest hindrance. Only what he called a "tremendous metamorphosis" on the part of the public could assure the development of a modern nation.

The work contains the usual abundance of sub-plots in the form of melodramatic love stories, but the historical narration is fairly well unified. It has more of real humanity than some of his earlier works.

The date of composition of *La majestad caída* was somewhere between May, 1911, and the close of 1913, for the work contains Diaz' letter of resignation, which was dated May 25, 1911, and Mateos died December 29, 1913.

This work is decidedly inferior to his other works. Poor form, strained eloquence, insipid love-making, abrupt and forced denouements, substitution of caricature for character study and empty dramatic thunder abound in the work. His climaxes would have been effective if he had built up the situation for their acceptance, but such was not the case. The cheering of the people was

> . . . un grito terrible, como si saliera de los antros del planeta. Grito que estremeció la tierra mexicana.[1]

Other examples of oratorical tone are:

> En medio de la noche oscura de los siglos despuntó la primera luz de un sol inmortal, en las montañas de oro de Guanajuato, que alumbró los altares de la patria a cuyas plantas se arrojó la generación actual . . .[2]

> ¡Puebla! la patria de la belleza; la cuna del valor y del heroísmo . . .¡ Puebla! . . . la que lleva sobre

---

[1]Juan A. Mateos: *La majestad caída,* México, Maucci Hnos., n. d., p. 8.

[. . . a terrible shout, as if it came from the deep caverns of the planet. A shout that shook the Mexican nation.]

[2]*Ibid.,* p. 6.

[In the dead of the dark night of the centuries there dawned the first light of an immortal sun, in the golden mountains of Guanajuato, which illumined the altars of the fatherland at whose feet the present generation threw itself . . .]

su osada frente los laureles de Santa Inés y Pitiminí . . .[1]

In addition to the works described, Mateos wrote: *Sor Angélica. Memorias de una hermana de la caridad*, 1875, *Los dramas de México*, 1887, *Las olas altas*, 1899, *La baja marea. Continuación de Las olas altas*, 1899, *El vendedor de periódicos. Tercera parte de Las olas altas*, 1899, *Las olas muertas. Cuarta parte de Las olas altas*, 1899, *Sangre de niños, Primer año del siglo xx*, 1901, and *Sepulcros blanqueados*, 1902.

These works are not sufficiently different from those discussed to make necessary their analysis within the limits imposed on this dissertation.

PASCUAL ALMAZÁN

Using the pseudonym Natal del Pomar, Almazán published the only edition of *Un hereje y un musulmán* in 1870. It is strange that this novel had only one edition and that

---

[1]*Ibid.*, p. 72.

[Puebla! the homeland of beauty; the cradle of valor and of heroism . . . Puebla! . . . she who wears on her brave forehead the laurels of Saint Inés and Pitiminí.]

some of the works of Riva Palacio and Juan A. Mateos had several editions, for it is superior to anything either of the other two authors wrote. González Obregón considered Almazán among the best historical novelists of Mexico up to 1889.[1]

The action of *Un hereje y un musulmán* begins in 1569 in the neighborhood of Papantla, Vera Cruz. The story is as follows:

Adriano Dolmos, son of Teófilo Dolmos, of Flemish descent, returned from Europe after finishing his education. With him he brought his teacher, Dr. Gutherzig, a profound scholar of Lutheran training and of deeply religious philosophy. Soon after his arrival Adriano fell in love with his cousin, Elvira, who had lived with his father since the death of her own parents.

Don Juan Alavez, a familiar of the Inquisition, held land adjoining the *encomienda* of Dolmos. Though an informant of the *Santo Oficio,* this Alavez was a Moor who was plotting to establish in the northern part of the state of Vera Cruz a colony for the Moors exiled from

---

[1] Luis González Obregón: *Breve noticia de los novelistas mexicanos en el siglo xix,* p. 31.

Spain in 1492.   His plan was to throw off the
yoke of Spain and establish an independent
state after the Moorish settlement gained a foot-
hold.

In order to carry out his plan, Alavez killed
the elder Dolmos and accused the son of heresy
before the Inquisition.   During the two years
Adriano was in prison, Alavez tried unsuccess-
fully to break the will of Elvira. His crime and
heresy were discovered in time to save the honor
of Elvira and the life of Adriano, and he himself became the victim of the institution he had
tried to use as an instrument for the extermination of the Dolmos family.

Some of the chapters of this book taken sep-
arately are convincing and impressive. Chapter
III, for example, carries a good picture of the
honest heretical thinker of the sixteenth century.
He was a saintly old man whose greatest crime
was too much understanding of and sympathy
for humanity, and too much tolerance. He was
too great to be a fanatic, but lived, unfortunately, in an age that demanded fanaticism. That he
was not a partisan of any religious group is
shown by the fact that he rejected the attitudes
of Luther and Calvin as well as those of the

Roman ecclesiastics. He considered them all too much the victims of authoritarianism. He denounced the idea of God as an arbitrary being; and he saw the superiority of many pagan conceptions over the kind of Christianity practiced in that time. He refused to concede that the comparatively recent religious ideas were superior to the more ancient, using as an illustration that the farther water flows from the spring, the more contaminated it becomes.

This interesting character was an humble but enthusiastic student of nature whose gradually weakening religious faith had left him mildly agnostic as to man's ultimate fate. His intellectual honesty stands out in striking contrast to the spirit of the times. When asked why he did not remember his faith as a child and return to the orthodox position, he replied:

> Se puede mandar en la memoria, se inclina la voluntad, pero sólo la locura puede alterar la inteligencia.[1]

Because he hated all intolerance, he could accept neither the fanaticism of the controlling re-

---

[1]Pascual Almazán: *Un hereje y un musulmán*, México, 1870, pp. 31-32.

[One may command his memory, one may bend his will, but only insanity may alter intelligence.]

ligious group nor that of the reformers. Both
groups, in his mind, were guilty of the same fun-
damental error. He was therefore anathema to
both Catholic and Protestant. This man is a
synthetic being made up of the author's own
ideals.

But he is the only character developed in the
novel. The others make little impression, because they are stereotyped. There are some attempts to incorporate local color into the work,
but they are not sustained and are never quite
successful. The author evidently realized the
importance of this element in the novel, probably because of the teachings of Altamirano,
but he was unable to make his plot fit into a realistic background.

There is abundant interpretative criticism,
sometimes severely satirical, of society of the
times. In satirizing the religious practices of
the day the author presented a priest exorcizing
an approaching storm. In explaining why the
storm came on in spite of his exorcisms the
priest's assistant informed his master that
through his ignorance of Latin he had exorcised
el pulgón, or vine-fretter, and that the palms,
with which the *lignum crucis* used in the cere-

mony had been made, had not been properly blessed on Palm Sunday.

The work contains interesting, though not numerous, recreations of colonial times. The daily manners of life, including such items as the habit of drinking chocolate among the wealthy as a means of escaping the boredom that came from leisure, have a ring of genuineness.

In nearly all his attacks on the institutions existing in Mexico, the author is artist enough to merge the abuses with the spirit of the times. He cited similar abuses in France and in Salem, in order to show that other races and religious groups were guilty of the same attitudes. The depths of universal ignorance of the epoch pre-occupied the author rather than specific injustices.

This is the second Mexican historical novel that gives interesting treatment of piracy, the first being *El filibustero* of Eligio Ancona. The author presents the denizens of the Gulf of Darien, the crews of John Morgan, of John Hawkins, of Francis Drake, of Thomas Cavendish, Roch, and Lolonois. The lives of John Morgan, Hawkins, and Drake are reviewed briefly.

The style of *Un hereje y un musulmán* is simple and clear. Its calmness, even when the subject matter demands tension, is a relief from the style of Mateos and Riva Palacio.

Paz' first novel, *La piedra del sacrificio,* was published in 1871 in two volumes of 311 and 219 pages respectively. The second edition appeared in 1874 and the third in 1881. *Amor y suplicio* has four editions listed in Iguíniz' *Bibliografía de novelistas mexicanos,* one of which bears no date, the other three dated 1873, 1881, and 1898-1899 respectively. The last mentioned edition was called the seventh by the publishers. Neither Iguíniz nor Torres-Rioseco gives any indication as to the dates of the other three editions. Paz' other novelistic works are *Amor de viejo* with one edition in 1874 and one in 1882, *Guadalupe* likewise with one edition in 1874 and another in 1882, *Doña Marina,* 1883, and thirteen historical novels called *Leyendas históricas* with a total of more than 6100 pages.

Amor y suplicio, according to a letter written by the author to José María Vigil and printed in the foreword of this work, was finished in 1866. The first part of it was read in sessions of the *Ensayo Literario.*

This story opens with a scene of primeval beauty in the forests surrounding Tenochtitlán, the Aztec capital. "Corpulent trees dressed with tender foliage," "perfumed shadows," "blue ivy," "wild jazmines," "thousands of birds bedecked in varied plumage," sweet warblings, "the mysterious murmur of a brook that wound, stumbling over rocks," a swan that rocked voluptuously, bidding goodbye to the falling evening, a young Indian hunter of royal blood seeking relief from sadness in the forests, vaguely melancholy, preoccupied, beautiful of body, mind and soul—these and many others suggest the influence of Esteban Echevrría, of Jorge Isaacs, and of Chateaubriand. With the latter Paz would say concerning the first part of *Amor y suplicio*: "Peignons la nature, mais la belle nature."[1] It is probable that the literary doctrines of Ignacio Manuel Altamirano were more immediately responsible for this emphasis on local color, for they had become

---

[1] Preface to Chateaubriand's *Atala.*
[Let us paint nature, but beautiful nature.]

known to practically all Mexican writers by the time this book was written. To Paz, as to Rousseau, there was a special attraction in the contemplation of primitivism in human beings and in nature unspoiled by civilization. The former was free, however, from the libertinism of many European romantics; the young Amerind lovers were as void of concupiscence as Longfellow's *Evangeline* and as natural as Bernardin de St. Pierre's characters in *Paul et Virginie.*

A suggestion of the spirit of the old epics of Spain is found in the actions of Cuauhtémoc in seeking an interview with Otila, the daughter of Maxixcatzín, Governor of the Tlaxcaltecans, who, being mortal enemies of the Aztecs, would certainly sacrifice him to their gods if he were discovered. The bold young man entered the palace of Maxixcatzín on the occasion of a great feast. Forced to reveal his identity or permit himself to be insulted, Cuauhtémoc made himself known, and challenged the general of the Tlaxcaltecan army to a duel. Like the Moor in *Historia del Abencerraje y la hermosa Jarifa,* he won the admiration of his enemies and ultimately his freedom.

From the coming of the Spaniards the story relies more and more on the facts of history for its framework. Thereafter the daring deeds of the small group of Spaniards and their allies, constantly threatened with annihilation, is the stirring theme of the first volume of *Amor y suplicio*.

The second volume continues the story of the conflict between the Spaniards and the Aztecs until the last of the Montezumas had died and the Amerinds were completely conquered. The bravery and the determination of Cortés and the desperate, futile courage of the Aztecs are the main theme. Cuauhtémoc, Xicoténcal and Otila, who had been baptized with the name Elvira, and who had married Juan Velásquez de León, carry the romance.

The daring, the duplicity and the cruelty of Cortés are much the same as they were pictured by Eligio Ancona in *Los mártires del Anáhuac*. Montezuma, pictured by Ancona as a weak, sentimental moron, is presented in Paz' work as a proud, strong and haughty monarch, possessed of a personality that made Cortés tremble when

in his presence.[1] His superstition and natural
love of ease, however, kept him from taking a
definite stand soon enough to avert disaster. In
this connection Paz quotes Clavigero to the effect that Montezuma had been a fierce warrior
in his youth,[2] but that domestic delights and
superstitions had softened him to such an extent
that his subjects thought he had changed sex.

There are many episodes in this novel that are
not convincing; for instance, Cuauhtémoc, after
seeing thousands of his people slain, others
starved, betrayed, tortured and even burned alive
by the Christians, and while waiting for the
hour of his own execution at the hands of the
white men, is made to accept the religion of
these newcomers as the purest, kindest, and most
beautiful of all religions.

The style of the work is not distinctive in any
way; it is simple, somewhat monotonous, always
directly narrative.   There are no subtleties, no
attempt at variety, no unique charm of language
and few interesting sidelights; but though plain
and dull, the language is in keeping with the

---

[1]Ireneo Paz: *Amor y suplicio,* 7th. ed., México, 1898,
Vol. II, pp. 80-81.

[2]*Ibid.,* Vol. II, pp. 331-342.

author's conception of the novel as a story reeled off like a ball of yarn.

Doña Marina, the sequel to *Amor y suplicio,* deals with the period immediately following the destruction of the Aztec empire. The principal characters are Doña Marina, Cortés and his wife, Catalina, and a few surviving members of the house of Montezuma.

References and quotations given in the course of the novel indicate Paz' acquaintance with the most available histories of the conquest period, especially the *Cartas de relación,* and *Residencia contra Cortés,* Motolinia's *Historia de los Indios,* the works of Clavigero, Gómara, Díaz del Castillo, and Bartolomé de las Casas.

Doña Marina is a story of Marina's services to Cortés during the period of clashing ambitions of his friends and his enemies. She is pictured as his wise counselor and guardian angel. The second volume injects Catalina, Cortés' wife, into the story. After her arrival Cortés was forced to drive Doña Marina from his house. Catalina, a woman of low birth and of crude manners, entered into the political plots of the period, and made life so miserable for her husband that he killed her. Later when

Cortés married a Spanish lady of high standing, Marina killed herself.

There are many defects in *Doña Marina,* some of which seem unpardonable even in that period; for example, the weakness of such characters as Cuauhtlizin, who fawned at the feet of Doña Marina, though he knew she was partly responsible for the destruction of his people; the destruction of unity of plot by the introduction of a number of love affairs; such foolish situations as that of men unsheathing their daggers in the presence of their lovers, threatening to kill themselves if their love were not returned. Paz lacked judgment in the selection of his material, and he was unable to give progressive order to his narrative.

Of the thirteen *Leyendas históricas* of Ireneo Paz, the first six are called *Leyendas históricas de la independencia.* The list is as follows: *El Licenciado Verdad, La Corregidora, Hidalgo, Morelos, Mina, Guerrero, Antonio Rojas, Manuel Lozada, su Alteza Serenísima, Maximiliano, Juárez, Porfirio Díaz,* and *Madero.*

The procedure of Paz in the collection of material for this series of historical stories was not essentially different from that used by

Olavarría y Ferrari in his *Episodos nacionales mexicanos*. He merely selected from available histories and popular accounts the framework for his stories and injected a slight fictional factor for the sake of interest. A list of historical sources mentioned by him and a study of the origins of materials whose source he does not mention reveal the fact that his work was merely an adaptation and popularization of well-known works. In the tenth episode, dealing with Maximilian, the author stated that he had constantly by him the works of the following authors: Zamacois, Vigil, Rivera Cambas, Pruneda, Lefevre, Kératry, Hans, Basch, Payno, Dr. Rivera, Arias, Hijar y Haro, Martínez de la Torre, and Riva Palacio.

On page thirty-three of *La Corregidora* Paz gives figures for the amount of money sent to Spain by Garibay, which figures are given by Alamán in his *Historia de México*, Vol. I, page 286. Citations of Alamán are numerous; for example, *Morelos*, page 140, *Guerrero*, pages 163, 347, 350, and 366. In *Mina*, pages 288 and 307, Paz quotes some of Mina's proclamations and offers other material which he probably took from Alamán: *op. cit.*, IV, page 555;

Bustamante: *Cuadros históricos,* IV, pages 317-323, and 328-333; and Zamacois: *Historia de México,* 1879, X, page 254, The cat episode, *Mina,* pages 295-308, agrees essentially with Bustamante's account given in *ut sup.,* IV, page 340. The story of the attack made by the Insurgents on Apodaca at the hacienda of *Virreyes* was taken from Cavo: *Los tres siglos de México durante el gobierno español,* etc., page 366 of the *Suplemento.*[1]   Paz' account of the bravery of Pípila in setting fire to the door of the *Alhóndiga* in Guanajuato, given in *Hidalgo,* page 137, is adapted from Bustamante: *ut sup.,* I, page 39.[2]   His version of the betrayal of Hidalgo, Allende, and Aldama by Juan Garrido and the interception of the warrants for the arrest of Aldama and Allende sent out by Riaño coincides in substance with that of Mora in *México y sus revoluciones,* IV, pages 18-19. The report Paz gives in *Hidalgo,* pages 48-51 concerning Venegas' collection of money for the royal treasury in return for honors and

---

[1]Published in Mexico by J. R. Navarro, 1852.   The *Suplemento* was written by Bustamante.

[2]Both Alamán and Liceaga deny the details of Bustamante's account.

decorations was taken from *Gaceta de México,* 1810, I, pages 764-765, 776-786 and from *Diario de México,* XIII, pages 347-348. Some of the information concerning the forces of Hidalgo at the beginning of his march, given in *Hidalgo,* page 35, was taken from Negrete: *México en el siglo xix,* II, pages 19-20.

Some idea as to the authenticity of Paz' accounts may be gained by comparison of the following: Bancroft: *op. cit.,* IV, pages 46-47 and Paz: *El Licenciado Verdad,* pages 96-100 on the meeting of the *junta,* August 9, 1808; Hernández y Dávalos: *Colección de documentos,* I, page 511 and Paz: *ut sup.,* page 153 on the petition of the Mexican consulate to the viceroy to forbid the printing and distribution of pasquinades in Mexico, dated August 6, 1808; Bancroft: *op. cit.,* pages 48-49 and Paz: *ut sup.,* pages 156-162 on the dispute over the authority of the Spanish *juntas*; Bancroft: *op. cit.,* pages 48-49 and Paz: *ut sup.,* page 177 on Aguirre's suggestion that the authority of the *Junta de Sevilla* be recognized in the War and Treasury Departments, and Rayas' objection to that suggestion; Bancroft: *op. cit.,* page 49, footnote, and

Paz: *ut sup.*, pages 181-182 on the disposition Iturrigaray made of this problem.[1]

The fictional part of *El Licenciado Verdad*, first of the episodes, is of little interest. Its kneeling, eloquent swains and its heroines of knighthood days are thoroughly artificial. Both the material and its treatment are pointless and trite. There is more blending of the historical and the fictional factors than in the works of Olavarría y Ferrari, but not enough to justify the assignment of considerable literary merit to this work.

La Corregidora is a continuation without interruption of *El Licenciado Verdad*. It deals with the development of the movement for independence, encouraged by the uncertainty of political affairs in the mother country. The terroristic activities of the Inquisition, the arbitrary acts of the Board of Public Safety, Hidalgo's intellectual independence and scholarship, and the courage of Josefa Ortiz, wife of the *corregidor* Domínguez, are the most interesting phases of the work.

---

[1]Bancroft gave as his sources the following: Cancelada: *Verdad sabida*, pp. 36-37; Cavo: *Tres siglos*, etc., III, p. 235; Guerra: *Historia de la revolución de Nueva España*, I, p. 93.

The third story of the series, called *Hidalgo,* begins with the arrival of the Viceroy Venegas in Mexico City and ends with the execution of Hidalgo. It gives a fairly satisfactory interpretation of the revolutionary movement and of the states of mind of the various factions of the period. The long military campaign with its shifting fortunes occupies most of the 532 pages of the story. The historical details are presented in their proper perspective, with constant preoccupation to give expression to the basic idealism of the author. Chapters in which the author departs from the style and material of popularized history and gives a truly novelistic treatment to characters are, however, few. Chapter v, dealing with the wounded pride of the fallen *oidor* Aguirre, contains some effective character analysis. The usual trite, commonplace love affairs with their clandestine meetings, tragic conflicts and heroism contain nothing of true human relationships.

In brief, though the work is superior to Riva Palacio's work and is less bombastic than Mateos', and though it is less sketchy and has less of the formal tone of history than Olavarría's historical stories, its value as a novel is slight. Its only merit is that it is a fair relation and description in a popular vein of the fight for independence.

The fourth story of the group, *Morelos*, begins with an interesting bit of regionalism. The hut of an humble Indian is well described. All the first chapter is devoted to treatment of regional aspects. The attitude and procedure of Morelos are handled in a truly novelistic manner without resort to the quotation of documents and other historical material; but the author was not able to continue in this vein, and soon reverted to the colorless semi-historical narration characteristic of the preceding episodes.

The fifth of the series is an account of the expedition of Francisco Javier Mina. The minute tracing of the career of this character furnishes an unwieldly mass of information impossible of proper assimilation.

With *Guerrero* Paz brought the first series of his historical stories to an end. Judged by present standards the entire group is unsatisfactory as fiction. Its failure is discoverable in the erroneous motives that moved the author to write. According to his own statement, his purpose was:

. . . enaltecer como se merecen los hechos heroicos de nuestros antepasados, grabar en el corazón del pueblo los magníficos episodios de aquella terrible época, dar a conocer . . . el carácter y las tendencias de los personajes que en ella figuraron y contribuir dentro de la órbita de nuestras facultades, a la difusión de esta clase de conocimientos que no sólo sirven para vigorizar el ánimo con los recuerdos patrióticos, sino que forman así mismo la experiencia de las naciones.[1]

Paz lamented the fact that the stories of the first series had to be published by chapters which many times he did not have time to correct because of the haste with which they had to be finished.

The most serious fault of the entire group of stories of the first series is the author's attempt to parade in full focus before the reader numerous characters most of whom should have been used only to furnish background. Because he

---

[1]Ireneo Paz: *Leyendas históricas,* 2nd ed., México, 1885-1902, Series II, Vol. I, prologue, pp. 3-4.

[. . . to give merited exaltation to the heroic deeds of our forefathers, to engrave on the hearts of the people the magnificent events of that terrible epoch, to make known . . . the character and the feelings of the men who figured in it and to contribute in so far as we can to the diffusion of this kind of knowledge which not only serves to invigorate the soul with patriotic memories, but also comprises the experience of nations.]

was unable to distinguish between characters to be treated in detail and those who were to play minor roles, he attempted to use them all as major characters. The result is that a reader not already well acquainted with the details of the period is unable to orient the characters and events presented.

In *Antonio Rojas,* the first of the second series, Paz evidently attempted to remove some of the weaknesses of the first series. The inordinate amount of purely historical material is reduced, and there is a tendency to limit the work to a narrow field with more attention to fiction. As a rule, the stories of the second series are shorter than those of the first, they do not follow so rigidly a chronological order, and they do not attempt to include all the movements and characters of the periods described; but though these changes improve the value of Paz' work as a novelist, they are not carried sufficiently far to result in an entirely satisfactory technique. Another improvement is to be found in the increased emphasis on local color.

In *Manuel Lozada,* the second story of the second series, for the first time Paz achieved unity in this group of historical novels, and for the first time he narrowed and defined his purpose sufficiently to permit of good literary work. The hoards of background figures continue to pass by the reader as before, but only in dim outline. The three main characters are nearly always in the foreground, acting in a medium partially created by the vaguely visible scores of minors. In this work the fictional material is more nearly true fiction, though of rather realistic trend; the main characters are weak and selfish, sensual and materialistic, unscrupulous and opportunistic, vengeful, jealous, murderous, occasionally softened by love and kindness, but usually as unsocial as any like group could be expected to be in a predatory society.

Lozada was the crude, unlettered leader of a gang of bandits who, though always the same in nature and activities, were given different political labels with every change in political leadership. At first they were called bandits, later they were guards for a firm of smugglers, then they were given the standing of regular troops by the conservatives and imperialists. After the triumph of the liberals they were again rightly called bandits. For the entire period of nearly twenty years they were nothing more than outlaws of the most vicious sort.

The general impression of desolation in the physical aspects of regions ravaged by the bandits is fairly definite, not because of detailed description, but by stimulation of the imagination with the description of the acts of the raiders.

Manuel Lozada is much like Azuela's *Los de abajo* in general tone. In it there is good portrayal, though not so vividly done as in *Los de abajo*. The work follows the procedure recommended constantly by Altamirano, and later illustrated by him in *El Zarco*; namely, the faithful portrayal of Mexican types and scenery.

The third legend of the second series is called *Su Alteza Serenísima*. It is a rambling account of the life of Santa Anna, with considerable space given to love affairs that have nothing to do with the main theme. The style is barren and uninteresting.

In *Maximiliano* Paz returned to the style and procedure of his earlier works. In the introduction to this work he wrote that his aim was to write a popular history of the period.

. . . sin apartarme ni un ápice de la historia, sin cambiar en su esencia los acontecimientos, sin alterar para nada la verdad . . .[1]

Es la misión que tienen que llenar todos los cronistas arrojar el baldón sobre los malos, sobre los pérfidos, sobre los criminales, y hacer el pedestal para que descanse sobre él la gloria de los buenos.[2]

DEMETRIO MEJÍA

"Entre el amor y la patria is the tribute of love that I wanted to pay my country" is the author's statement of his motive in writing his only novel. And the work is just that. Intense patriotism pervades it. As the ardent lover of his country Mejía painted her in a glow that at times warms the reader to sympathy.

There is one section of this novel, that in which Mejía tells of the journey of Luis and Margarita through the mountainous region from

---

[1]Ireneo Paz: *Maximiliano*, México, 1899, p. 4.

[. . .without departing in the minutest detail from history, without changing the essential nature of facts, without making any alteration of the truth for any purpose.]

[2]*Ibid.*, p. 5.

[It is the mission that all chroniclers have to fulfill to heap insult on the wicked, on the perfidious, on the criminal, and to make a pedestal in order that the glory of the good may rest on it.]

the *Hacienda del Rincón* to Teotitlán, that contains some very attractive landscape painting. Of particular beauty is the description of Zoquiapam and the sea coast seen from the mountain peaks. This part of the novel is worth preserving as a short descriptive sketch. It reminds one strongly of parts of Altamirano's *La navidad en las montañas*.

CHAPTER IV

THE BEGINNING OF REALISTIC AND NAT-
URALISTIC INFLUENCES

With the definite triumph of the reform
movement in 1867 under the leadership of
Benito Juárez, there began in Mexico a period
of tranquility that was to last with comparatively few interruptions until 1910. Soon after
1867 political animosities were lessened by a
general amnesty granted to the leaders of the
defeated imperialists. Ignacio Manuel Altamirano, always concerned with the development
of a national literature and conscious of the ef-
fects of political passion on literary art, under-
took the task of turning the minds of writers of
all political faiths toward literary creation. In
the columns of *El Renacimiento* (1869) he invited the colaboration of "all lovers of belles
lettres" of "all political communions." Under
the guidance of this magnanimous critic men
who had been political enemies fraternized in
literary clubs. Manuel Payno, whose death
Altamirano himself had demanded in a passionate oration before the national congress in 1861,
and such staunch imperialists as Roa Bárcena

worked in harmony with ardent liberals, even with Ignacio Ramírez, the bitterest critic of the conservative regime.

In 1875 was founded the *Academia Mexicana* as a correspondent of the *Real Academia Española,* under whose encouragement and guidance it initiated a movement to purge Mexican Spanish of its corruptions and to establish sound literary doctrines.

For the first time in the history of independent Mexico there existed among writers a widespread realization of the necessity for careful study of the criteria of literary art. This realization led to the serious analysis of the works of Spanish, French, Italian, German and English authors. It will be recalled that during the first part of the nineteenth century there had existed a curiosity concerning foreign thought trends; but that interest was limited to the philosophical, social and political attitudes of European thinkers and to their procedure in general. It was not sufficiently analytical of detailed technique. The interest that the writers of the post-reform period had in foreign literatures and in that of their mother country was critical of details both of content and of form.

Nor was the study of the latter group directed toward imitation; it had as its motive the development of skill and aesthetic discernment to be applied to the interpretation of national life.

In their search for guidance Mexican novelists naturally turned first to Spain. There they found their most important orienting force, the traditional realism of Spanish literature and thought. Benito Pérez Galdós, José María de Pereda, Juan Valera and Emilia Pardo Bazán became their masters. Emilio Rabasa's work, for example, shows clearly the influence of Pérez Galdós in both form and interpretative procedure, and José López Portillo y Rojas, especially in *La parcela*, reveals a debt to Pereda in the matter of minute observation and regional dialogue.

Toward the end of the century the influence of French naturalists became rather pronounced. The influence of Emil Zola and of the Goncourts is clearly seen in Federico Gamboa's technique and in his tendency to paint the repugnant aspects of life. As will be shown later, Manuel Martínez de Castro and Manuel Payno followed at times the example set by Zola in reducing the individual to a complex of forces susceptible of minute scientific analysis.

Attention should be called to the fact that these developments in literature did not follow immediately the triumph of the reform movement. They took more the course of gradual evolution than that of sudden revolution. Not before the eighties were they well established. Nor can it be said that romanticism disappeared with the appearance of these new trends. The romantic movement persisted, not as it had been, violent, incorrect, noisy and exaggerated, but purified and sincere.

MANUEL MARTÍNEZ DE CASTRO

Martínez de Castro's novel *Eva,* published in 1885, though not purely historical in nature, has enough of historical background to justify its inclusion in this study. What the author considered to be the iniquitous injustices of the age of Santa Anna and of the period of the French occupation, and the curse of the military factions with their debauched personnel and inhuman methods of conscription furnish the background for the story.

The work is a peculiar mixture of romanticism and crass realism imitated from the then new naturalistic school of France. It contains significant evidence of the infiltration of naturalism into Mexican fiction.

The attempt to apply the procedure of Zola's school is clear in the detailed study of the gradual change of Eva's attitudes after her rape by a group of soldiers. Deprived of virtue and social status through no fault of her own, and unable to marry an honorable man, she at first secluded herself; but meditation on the injustice of life inevitably produced a steadily increasing hardening of her naturally docile character until at last she became obsessed with the desire for vengeance on all mankind. That her coquetry caused the death of several innocent admirers and left her kind and unsuspecting fosterfather to pay with his life for the death of her last victim did not trouble her. The idealism of the shy maiden had been transformed into a predatory malevolence.

A pitiful and often gruesome character is Ogli, Eva's brother, who was hideously deformed. Ogli was a noble soul; he had attempted from infancy to protect his orphan sister, giving her food without tasting it himself when both

were starving. His infancy and childhood had
been a courageous fight in her behalf; but his
deformities incapacitated him for profitable em-
ployment. His failure to bear adequately the
responsibility of providing for his sister and
his inability to defend her against the attack of
licentious soldiers of Mejía's *Army of the Cross*
crushed him. The constant realization that life
had dealt an unspeakably cruel fate to both of
them embittered him to such a degree that he
came to despise society and all of its conventionalities. The common plight of the two drew
them closer together.

Ogli, unable to interest other women because
of his hideous figure, and impressed with Eva's
enforced loneliness, conceived an incestuous
love as the solution of his own and Eva's problems. But his improper proposal made him ab-
horrent to her. Realizing then the enormity of
his crime, he sought to bury himself in his
foster-father's laboratory, seeking escape from
life in the study of science. He became atheistic
and hard. For him only the mechanics of natural
laws existed; all else was illusion.

If this novel had confined itself to the study
of these two characters, and had included only

the material necessary to develop them it would have been much improved. As it is, it contains most of the defects of prior Mexican fiction, namely: useless length, pompous style in conversation, extraneous material, absence of *costumbrista* material, lack of adaptation of thought to the condition of the characters, and lack of stylistic merit. There is present in the work, however, a nascent sense of the desirability of close observation and technical detailed study of individuals.

Martínez de Castro wrote also *Julia,* a historical novel in two volumes, published in 1868 and again in 1874; *Una Madre i una hija,* a novel of 142 pages published in 1875; and *Elvira* published in 1889.

MANUEL PAYNO

Forty-three years after the appearance of the first chapters of *El fistol del diablo,* Payno started publication of *Los bandidos de Río Frío* in Barcelona under the pseudonym *Un ingenio de la corte.* Dr. J. R. Spell places the date of composition at the year 1882 while Payno was in Spain.[1] Solórzano del Valle, in a critical

---

[1] J. R. Spell: *The Literary Works of Manuel Payno,* in *Hispania,* 1929, Vol. XII, pp. 347-356.

foreword to the first volume, stated that publication was started in Barcelona in 1888, and the author's prologue bears the latter date. The novel was probably not finished until three years later, for at the end of the second volume the author wrote:

> Termino, a Dios gracias, la inacabable novela de *Los bandidos de Río Frío*. Hotel de Rhin, Dieppe, julio, 1891.[1]

The work was printed in two volumes in 4⁰ with a total of 1991 pages. There was an edition printed in Mexico in 1919, and another in Buenos Aires and Mexico in 1927, and one was issued without date by La Casa Editorial Lozano, San Antonio, Texas.

This is by far the best work of Payno, and in several regards the best historical novel of the nineteenth century. In it the weaknesses of *El fistol del diablo* were greatly reduced, though not entirely removed, and the attractive features of that earlier work were intensified and improved in technique of presentation. The author again apologized for the many interruptions of his stories—and there are several stories

---

[1] [I now finish, thanks be to God, the interminable novel *Los bandidas de Río Frío*. Hotel de Rhin, Dieppe, July, 1891.]

carried along together––by the inclusion of didactic and philosophical digressions; but he ex-
cused himself, stating that he was not trying to
write a novel comparable in interest to the best
novels of France, Spain and England, but was
interested rather in describing the scenes of
every-day life among his people, in recording
customs that were disappearing, and sketching
faithfully the individuals "that had died . . .
the buildings that had been torn down."[1]

In the scintillating realism of the numerous
episodic fragments composing a veritable panorama of Mexican life lies the art of Payno. It
is to his credit that he did not try to imitate more
sophisticated authors in plot interest and that
he did not strive after generic breadth. His
characters are definite, breathing, specific individuals whose type characteristics are inci-
dental, not made-to-order specimens. He had
the philosophical breadth to place his art on a
plane above the level of group animosities and
fanaticism.

In the matter of detailed portrayal Payno had
learned much from the study of the works of

---

[1]Manuel Payno: *Los bandidos de Río Frío*, México and
Buenos Aires, Maucci Hnos., n. d., Vol. I, p. 140.

foreign authors, especially from the French realists and naturalists, some of whom he knew personally during his stay in Europe. The care with which the latter worked out the minutiae of background and their attempt to apply the technique of science in the formation of their reaction patterns were consonant with tendencies Payno had shown from the first, though in rather amateurish fashion. This influence is strikingly clear in the development of Evaristo's character;[1] in the drunken brawls of artisans on Holy

---

[1]When he was first introduced Evaristo was a poor but honest wood-carver, living in natural union with Casilda. His environment and a series of social injustices antagonized him and aroused predatory propensities that finally came to govern all his attitudes. His first hostile acts were directed at offenders only; but as he grew increasingly egocentric, every human being became fair prey. Losing all sense of gratitude to his mate for her faithfulness, he tired of her and planned to be rid of her by drowning her in the canal; but his cunning led him to take the safer course of beating her so often and offending her with so many indignities that she would leave of her own accord, a procedure so common among men of his class that it found expression in a popular phrase: *quererla y aburrirla*.

In order to meet Evaristo's demands for food Casilda worked doggedly and pawned her clothing. When she had nothing left to pawn, Evaristo became implacable. The final beating left her insensible and bloody.

Feelings of remorse for such cruelty to the one who

Monday,[1] ending in indecencies and crimes; in the habits of anti-social males, who while desiring cohabitation with decent women, used crim-

---

had patiently shared his poverty and had been his only friend for so long stirred in Evaristo the little good that was left as he watched her insensible form writhing in pain; but it was not strong enough to mend the wrong nor to change his attitude when Casilda regained consciousness. He drove her out and watched her stumble into the darkness, driven along by a bitterly cold wind, then turned his thoughts to Tules whom he had been wooing with costly presents.

Rid of Casilda, Evaristo married Tules, a refined girl in destitute circumstances. He was quickly driven to hate her because of the shock she sustained from his brutishness. Her superiority of character nettled him; and he despised her as he despised everything decent, because she gave him a sense of his own depravity. In a drunken stupor he killed her for not being able to buy food without money. Zola would have approved the scene in which Evaristo, drenched with Tule's blood, fell across her lifeless body, pressing against her bloodless lips his own pulque-reeking, vomit-besmeared mouth, thinking in his delirium that he was in the arms of another woman.

Recovered from his stupor, Evaristo killed Tules' pet kid and bore its dripping carcass into the street in order to explain satisfactorily the blood he had been unable to remove from his clothing and person. The good in him was then dead. He was at last the human beast whose subsequent acts would satisfy the most confirmed naturalist. Natural propensities stimulated by environment had done their work.

[1]*Ibid.*, Vol. I, chap. xix.

inal methods to remain *chinos libres*;[1] in the fight between buzzards and dogs over the body of a live child abandoned on the city dump heap;[2] in the interest in biology shown in the description of the habits of spiders;[3] in the description of the campaign to destroy stray dogs that infested the capital;[4] and in the human wrecks searching refuse piles for food.

---

[1] *Ibid.*, Vol. I, Chaps. XVI-XVIII, especially p. 125.

[2] A band of starving, homeless dogs came upon an infant that had been thrown on the refuse pile as an offering to an Indian goddess by an Indian herbalist. The dogs and vultures fought over the prey.

[3] Manuel Payno: *Los bandidos de Río Frío,* Vol. I, p. 96.

[4] In *ibid.*, Vol. I, Chap. x, Payno discusses the life of homeless dogs. He presents the custom shoemakers had of keeping always filled with water a bowl placed in front of their shops so the dogs could drink; the decree calling for the death of all dogs found on the streets at night; the zeal of the *serenos* in clubbing dogs, for each one of whose dead bodies they received one *real;* the bloody carcasses; the howling victims escaping with broken legs and ribs; the pitiful moans of the expiring; the procession of the *serenos* to headquarters in the mornings, dragging through the streets the bloody disfigured dogs tied together with ropes, finally dumping them in a heap before the chief of police, who commended them for their work and paid them the bounty agreed on. The accumulated carcasses were piled in a heap and exhibited as a public spectacle. The dogs finally forsook the city at night and took refuge in

In the *costumbrista* phases of this work the critic will find the repetition of the good qualities of *El fistol del diablo*, improved in taste and in minuteness of detail. Some of the scenes of *Los bandidos de Río Frío* are so faithfully and completely done that they are indispensable in the study of Mexican life of the past century. They surpass any formal treatise by professional historians and sociologists in the depiction of detailed background. Thoroughness requires the discussion of a few typical scenes.

Chapter XI of the first volume constitutes an excellent description of the canals and the buildings lining their shores; the rotting refuse of vegetable and animal origin; the contaminated water; the old houses with irregular balcony railings and heavy gratings; the boats filled with produce, including maize, barley, vegetables, fruits, flowers, and numerous other items; the host of flower retailers, coming for supplies, then scattering to the various parts of the city to sit on street corners exhibiting their wares; the Indian women, dressed in primitive costumes; the dirty stalls and stores of the first

la viña, the city dump-ground, returning to the city after daybreak to hunt food.

floors of the houses; the *tocinerías* with their pungent smells, their vessels filled with lard, cracklings, and fried meat, with their large ash cutting blocks and counters adorned with sacred images in whose honor candles are kept burning, and with strings of sausages and peppers hanging from rafters.

There are pulque shops where sodden brains brew dangerous fights and where heavily rouged robust girls painted on the walls incite disturbing reactions with ill concealed charms; there are feed stalls marked by tufts of straw hung over the front entrance where muleteers can buy hay for their mules and the poor may find beans for their children. The coal dealer in his hole--in-the-wall store showing his wares in dirty sacks set on the sidewalk, the wood sellers and scores of other dirty vendors of dirtier wares do thriving business with the ragged inhabitants of the slums.

Payno pictures this same section decorated for Good Friday celebrations. The streets were swept clean, the filth cleaned away; the water was filled with decorated boats loaded with flowers and the little bridges were covered with colored streamers.

Considerable space, beginning with page 117, is devoted to a detailed description of the fruit business, wholesale and retail, centered at the Puente de la Lana.

One of Payno's most effective pictures is that of *La Viña*, the capital's dump-ground. The mountainous rows of junk and filth rotting in the sun and giving off putrifactive gases which the wind carried over the city were the abodes of beggars, dogs, thieves, smugglers, homeless wretches and naked children, all sleeping by night in holes dug between the rows of junk and poking by day through each cart load of the refuse as it arrived, in search of bits of clothing, iron, broken dishes, and pieces of metal and wood, and competing with vultures for morsels of rotting food. At the end of this description the author indulged in one of his out-of-role-lectures in which he censured public officials for permitting such conditions to exist.

Brief mention should be made of other interesting details: the workshop of a cabinet maker and his dining room;[1] bandit methods in an at-

---

[1]Manuel Payno: *Los bandidos de Río Frío,* Vol. I, p. 145.

tack on a stage coach;[1] commerce on the canals;[2] street scenes at night;[3] gambling houses;[4] San Angel, the fashionable summer resort for the rich;[5] a day among Indians on farms, their work, their food and their animals trying to appease their hunger by licking each other;[6] the Indian village of Salinas where the aborigines led a primitive life, diseased and dying like wild dogs, treated only by native herbalists, burying their dead in pastures for want of money to pay the fees demanded by the Santa Ana parish;[7] peons living in huts of dirt and straw, tearing them down and rebuilding them wherever their labor demanded;[8] Indians mixing Christianity with their old superstitions, confusing Mary with the goddess Tonantzin, too deeply sunk in ignorance to understand the aestheticism and symbolism of Christianity;[9] the *macehuales* living by catching frogs and

---

[1]*Ibid.*, Chap. xlviii.
[2]*Ibid.*, Chaps. xxix-xxx.
[3]*Ibid.*, p. 80.
[4]*Ibid.*, Vol. II, pp. 242-249.
[5]*Ibid.*, Chap. xxiii.
[6]*Ibid.*, Vol. I, pp. 22-23.
[7]*Ibid.*, Vol. I, p. 35.
[8]*Ibid.*, p. 21.
[9]*Ibid.*, p. 46.

small fish, by snaring mosquitoes to sell as bird food, by gathering *ahuautle* and *tequesquite*, and by making salt from the lake water;[1] the improvidence of the poor who spent their money wildly when they had any, then returned to the fight against starvation;[2] and the aristocratic rich heaping injustices on the lower class.[3]

Though Payno did not sacrifice the individuality of his characters to the creation of types, the personnel of his work constitutes a summary of social forces and attitudes. Dedolla, for instance, was made to say:

> . . . el dinero es el alma del mundo. Sin dinero no es posible ni aún entrar a la gloria.[4]

An army officer remarked:

> El plan es ganar dinero por todos los medios posibles, robar en grande, ejercer . . . el monopolio del robo.[5]

---

[1]*Ibid.*, pp. 33-34.

[2]*Ibid.*, p. 121.

[3]*Ibid.*, Chap. xv.

[4]*Ibid.*, p. 331.

[Money is the soul of the world. Without it one cannot even enter heaven.]

[5]*Ibid.*, Vol. II, p. 312.

[My plan is to make money by all possible means, to rob at wholesale, to acquire . . . a monopoly of robbery.]

Relumbrón, a bandit chief and public official, expressed his attitude as follows:

> La mitad de todos los habitantes del mundo ha nacido para robar a la otra mitad, y esa mitad robada, cuando abre los ojos y reflexiona, se dedica a robar a la mitad que la robó y le quita no sólo lo robado, sino lo que poseía legalmente. Esta es la lucha por la vida.[1]

A lawyer spent his time stirring up suits with no basis of justice.[2] Various newspaper editors competed for government favor and for positions of rich rewards for little work.[3] *El eco del mundo*, a cheap journal, catered to one faction after another until it offended them all and had to turn to sensational crime news. After government support was withdrawn, it became inspired with patriotic zeal for reform in government.[4]

In Bedolla, Payno showed how a *caudillo* is developed. This individual became a conspira-

---

[1] *Ibid.*, p. 313.

[Half the people of the world were born to rob the other half, and the cheated half, when it opens its eyes and thinks, sets about robbing the half that robbed it and takes back, not only that which was stolen at first, but also that which was legally possessed by the original robbers . . . This is the fight for existence . . .]

[2] *Ibid.*, Vol. I, pp. 25-26.

[3] *Ibid.*, p. 20.

[4] *Ibid.*, pp. 327-329; also p. 110.

tor because he justly lost his political standing. Such disgruntled leeches as he, allied with criminal rings, were charged with the instigation of Mexican revolutions. In their *pronunciamientos* they posed as public-spirited heroes of sacred liberty, of the bleeding fatherland and even of religion.[1] The predatory nature of rebels fighting under pious banners is carefully drawn,[2] as are also the people who suffered abuses at the hands of the bandits, then swore they knew nothing when public authorities began an investigation.

The almost endless gallery of pictures includes the empty sham and perversion of military forces,[3] public graft,[4] the custom of clothing the most corrupt designs in religious pretense,[5] bribery,[6] the bungling of justice by news hounds and yellow journals,[7] the hasty opinions of the courts announced for political effect,[8]

---

[1]*Ibid.*, Vol. II, pp. 160-161 and 537.

[2]*Ibid.*, p. 225, and Chap. xxi.

[3]*Ibid.*, Chap. i; see also p. 96.

[4]*Ibid.*, Vol. I, p. 196. Chapters xxiv and xxv.

[5]*Ibid.*, Vol. II, p. 537.

[6]*Ibid.*, pp. 236, 238.

[7]*Ibid.*, Vol. I, Chap. xxvi, pp. 270, 284.

[8]*Ibid.*, p. 270.

and the passing of sentences of death on innocent people in order to satisfy the public demand
for a victim.[1]

In the treatment of crime as a major social
phenomenon Payno had the advantage of life-
long interest and study at home and abroad. He
was a criminologist with ideas that would now
be considered advanced. Criminality he considered to be largely the logical product of social institutions. The rapidly shifting political
governments took no interest in the training of
youth and the improvement of its environment;
they showed no concern that children were
thrown into close contact with chronic criminals
from whom they learned the technique of crime
and of corrupt political protection. Respect
for law, he charged, was impossible because of
the arbitrary injustice and even complicity in
crime of the judicial and executive departments.[2] Payno was sociologist enough to see
the relation between the treatment of criminals,

---

[1]*Ibid.*, p. 284.

[2]An example is found in Bedolla, the judge who demanded the death penalty for innocent defendants to
show the public he was a man of action.

especially children, and crime. He protested against the *Hospicio* in particular.[1]

In the contention that crime must continue to flourish until the education of the lower classes and the conditions in which they lived were improved Payno was in agreement with the views of such intelligent foreign observers as Brantz Mayer.[2] It was this class that furnished abundant material for bandit gangs and for revolutions.[3]

The church's failure to do its duty by this class was to him no less deplorable than the government's. The reproduction of a religious discussion among bandits, all of whom claimed to be devout Christians, and who believed that after a life of crime they could escape divine punishment by going through certain prescribed rituals, constitutes a stinging satire on religious instruction.[4]

---

[1]Manuel Payno: *Los bandidos de Río Frío*, Vol. I, p. 184.

[2]Brantz Mayer: *Mexico as it was and as it is*, New York, 1844, p. 42. "Is it wonderful in a city with an immense proportion of its inhabitants of such a class, hopeless in the present and in the future, that there should be murderers and robbers?"

[3]Manuel Payno: *Los bandidos de Río Frío*, Vol. II, pp. 76-79.

[4]*Ibid.*, pp. 322-323.

For education and scholarship of the period in question Payno had only profound disdain. He listed as follows the subjects taught: Latin, logic, metaphysics, laws, canons, "and other subjects fully as useful as this last"; and called attention to the need for a modern curriculum including modern languages, science and manual arts.[1] In telling the story of Juan he discussed the manner in which boys learned a trade: they were turned over to a tradesman as apprentices, and in many cases were reduced to a state of practical slavery.[2]

In a severely satirical vein Payno pictured the learned faculty of the University of Mexico called into consultation by Doctor Codorniú on the perplexing question of a woman's confinement of thirteen months without any sign of immediate parturition. The wise Doctor of Laws gave assurance that in the *Siete partidas,* in Solórzano and in the *Leyes de Indias* he could undoubtedly find information on the subject; the Doctor of Medicine was in favor of an exploratory operation; the Doctor of Theology gravely remarked: "Her count is wrong".

---

[1] *Ibid.,* Vol. I, p. 98.
[2] *Ibid.,* Chap. XII.

These deficiencies of the educational regime, elementary and advanced, Payno attributed to the domination of Mexico's intellectual life by dogmatism.[1] But space does not permit further discussion of institutional life and customs of the generation described.

Los bandidos de Río Frío is based on the career of Relumbrón, who was in real life Juan Yáñez, an artillery colonel and aide to Santa Anna, notorious in Mexican history as a business partner of thieves, robbers and bandits. He was military commander in Acatlán and held a responsible position in Puebla. His official and personal friendship with Santa Anna and his role as military commander gave him ample opportunity to keep up with the movements of merchandise and money on the highways, and afforded him protection from justice. His house was finally searched by the Conde de la Cortina with the result that a large quantity of plunder was found.

During his trial one of his prosecutors mysteriously died; popular belief was that Yáñez had him killed. The defendant and five of his confederates were condemned to death, but the

---

[1]*Ibid.*, p. 187.

former cut his own throat and died July 15, 1839.

Other historical characters are Santa Anna, Cordorniú, José Joaquín Pesado, Ignacio Cubas, Bernardo Couto, Manuel Escandón, José Villar, Lic. Zea, Lamparilla, Rodríguez de San Gabriel, Conde de San Diego del Sauz (in reality Conde de San Pedro del Álamo), and el Marqués de Valle Alegre. In the prologue Payno wrote that there were many socially and politically prominent persons involved in the affairs of Juan Yáñez whom he does not mention or whose identity he conceals. These individuals tried to stop the trial, but could not because the scandal had spread over Mexico to such an extent that popular indignation demanded action.

The weaknesses of the work are of the same nature, though less in degree, as those of *El fistol del diablo*. Payno attempted too much in one novel. Lack of unity was inescapable without severe trimming and reduction of material.

Both *El fistol del diablo* and *Los bandidos de Río Frío* have been ranked high by critics. Olavarría y Ferrari considered the former worthy of careful study for its realism and style.[1] J. R. Spell described Payno's style as "informal, intimate and chatty."[2] Altamirano listed Payno's characteristics as follows: unusual talent, fine observation, knowledge gained in travel and in the study of foreign works, and careful study of Mexican society.

González Peña considered Payno as a transition between the early Mexican novel and the novel of the second half of the century.[3] Federico Gamboa, speaking of *Los bandidos de Río Frío* said:

> . . . es obra mexicana por sus cuatro costados, sí obedece a plan preconcebido, luce unidad de acción y orientación recta, acrece con sabiduría y arte el léxico nuestro; incalculable es el número de mexicanismos . . . Deja harto atrás a *Periquillo* en todo y por todo, y a *Astucia* . . .[4]

---

[1]Olavarría y Ferrari: *El arte literaria en México*, 2nd. ed., p. 161.

[2]J. R. Spell: *op. cit.*, Vol. XII, p. 356. This article is one of the best on Payno.

[3]Carlos González Peña: *op. cit.*, p. 431.

[4]Federico Gamboa: *La novela mexicana*, México, 1914, p. 14.

> [. . . it is truly a Mexican work, it conforms to a preconceived plan, it has unity of action and proper orientation, it increases with knowledge and art our Mexican lexicon; the number of Mexicanisms is incalculable. It leaves both the *Periquillo* and *Astucia* far behind in every respect.]

Payno's superiority over Lizardi is attributable to his greater culture gained from travel and contact with foreign literature. He was a careful student of intellectual and literary movements abroad. In *El fistol del diablo* he mentioned the following: *El diccionario filosófico de Voltaire, El citador, La guerra de los Dioses, La doncella de Orleans, Lucinda, El Barón de Faublas, Las ruinas de Palmira, El hijo del Carnaval, Emilia, La profesión de fe del Presbítero Saboyano,* and the novels of Paul de Kock. He commented on Fénelon's description of the island of Calipso.[1] In addition to the French realists and naturalists it is certain that the works of Thierry, Walter Scott, Agnes Strickland, Hume, Smollet, Aikens, Labanoff were known to him, for on them he depended for guidance in the material of some of his short historical sketches. In *Los bandidos de Río Frío* he expressed high regard for such Americans as Washington, Adams, Cooper, Irving and Prescott.[2]

---

[1]Evidence of Fénelon's influence may be found in the description of Mexico's climate, *El fistol del diablo*, Vol. II, 1st and 2nd. pages of Chap. VII.

[2]Manuel Payno: *Los bandidos de Río Frío*, Vol. 1, p. 139.

Payno was encouraged in the tendency to give an important place to portrayal of customs by Altamirano, who was the outstanding champion of the *costumbrista* genre among Mexican critics. It must be remembered, however, that Payno started writing in this vein when Altamirano was a little boy. The influence of the "maestro" was one of encouragement and refinement of tastes. To Altamirano, called by González Peña "from a strictly literary point of view the first novelist . . . in the history of our letters . . .", is due some of the credit for improvement in Payno's technique and literary taste evident in *Los bandidos de Río Frío*.

HERIBERTO FRÍAS

The first novel written by Heriberto Frías was *Tomochic*. Both Iguíniz and Torres-Rioseco list four editions of this work, published as follows: 1894, 1906, 1911, and one edition without date. The edition of 1911 was called the fifth by the publishers.

The work deals with the revolt and subsequent annihilation of the religious and political fanatics of Tomochic during the campaign of Chihuahua in 1892. The long isolation in which the people of the region lived had resulted in the development of a religious cult with local saints and leaders. The latter used their prestige among the superstitious people for unmoral and selfish ends, with such abuses as concubinage in the family of the chief saint.

Cruz Chávez, the military leader of the town, had at his disposal a formidable group of fighters, most of them excellent marksmen renowned for their ability to kill one man with every bullet. Their ability, religious fanaticism and the untamed savage nature of the people made of them a dangerous foe. The hero, Miguel Mercado, is colorless and entirely unconvincing; but the rebels are interesting.

The battle of Tomochic is described in considerable detail, but the author was not capable of vivid terse description; his verbal equipment was not sufficient, and he seemingly knew nothing of the art of indirect description that is apparently secondary to action and speech, yet in reality is important in fiction. The style is journalistic, fairly well composed, but inelastic and without sparkle.

It is clear that at times the author was trying to follow several roads at once with no particular destination except the end of the book in mind. There is no unity, no plan, no balance, and very little judgment in the selection and rejection of material.

Las miserias de México continues the story of Mercado's life as hack writer for various newspapers of Mexico City after his more or less dishonorable discharge from the army occasioned by his inability to keep from telling the truth about military and political matters. The young man soon learned that writers of good faith, of originality and principle were not adapted to the demands of journalism, because Díaz had subdued the press to such an extent that dignified, honest newspaper men had been forced out of business.

In *El triunfo de Sancho Panza*, the third novel based on the life of Mercado, the character is presented as a journalist in Mazatlán. He is too Quixotic to be silent on the abuses he sees in the social order.

With defter treatment the picture of social life in Mazatlán presented by Frías would have been good literature; but as in *Tomochic* he lacked the finesse of technique that sometimes distinguishes art from near-art. This novel is superior to *Tomochic* in several ways: there is more unity, less dependence on unrelated and sensational plot fragments; there is closer attention to detail and a more constant consciousness of direction of movement than in *Tomochic*. There are in *El triunfo de Sancho Panza* some excellent pictures of social intrigue involving several realistic types, such as the gossip, the shyster lawyer, the quack physician, the clever promoter, the simple rich lamb ready to be shorn, the adulterous social aspirant, the honest Quixotic newspaper editor who is indiscreet enough to expose the corruption he saw in high places, and the whole set of public officials from Díaz down.

This work is expressive of the author's disillusionment. His faith in the ultimate triumph of good had been destroyed, as had also his belief in the basic goodness of humanity. His psychology of defeat left no ground for personal integrity and rendered futile in his thinking all effort aimed toward social uplift. To him it was useless to attempt to check the descent of humanity to constantly lower levels of degradation and depravity. Don Quijote was dead in him and only Sancho survived.

In 1899 Frías published *Leyendas históricas mexicanas*, a group of stories about the Amerinds before and immediately after the arrival of the Spaniards. Of them the author remarked:

> . . . darán a popularizar los más bellos episodios y las más curiosas costumbres de las primeras razas que habitaron el suelo de mi patria . . . A través de la ficción legendaria y tradicional que les prestan potente vida y amenidad, estarán al alcance de todas las inteligencias, que fué el principal objeto que me guió al escribir estas Leyendas.[1]

This group includes thirty-seven legends on the Amerinds of Mexico before the coming of the Spaniards and eight other short stories under the general heading *Cuentos históricos nacionales*. The average length of the stories is a little more than seven pages.

The first group deals with the wanderings of the various Amerind tribes, their fights with enemies under the protection of their several

---

[1]Heriberto Frías: *Leyendas históricas mexicanas,* Maucci, México, Barcelona, Buenos Aires, 1899, p. 5.

[. . . they will make known the most beautiful episodes and the most curios customs of the first races that inhabited the soil of my country . . . Through legendary and traditional fiction that gives them potent life and amenity they will be within the reach of all minds, which was the main object that guided me in writing these legends.]

gods, and their general tribal experiences with personal histories incident thereto.

But personal experiences of the characters are always secondary to destiny which over-shadows everything. This sense of destiny con-stitutes the author's interpretation of the mental and emotional life of all his characters.

> Sobre todas las razas que poblaron el Anáhuac desde los mas remotos ciclos de la historia tradicional y geroglífica, lapidaria y revelada en el misterio inviolable de los *teocallis,* sobre todos aquellos pueblos primitivos, aventureros y audaces, irradió desde un principio la soberana leyenda de sus profecías . . .
>
> ¡Era el terror del porvenir! ¡El formidable enigma de los acontecimientos futuros que habrían de engrandecer o aniquilar las razas, el incendio y desquiciamiento absoluto de sus naciones, se presentaba siempre ante los príncipes, los *tecuhtlis* y los sacerdotes del gran templo como la caída torrencial, negra, intangible y fantasmagórica de las aguas que de los altos cielos descienden arrastrando estrellas y precipitando a los abismos ignotos las naciones con sus reyes triunfadores y sus ídolos adorados . . .![1]

---

[1] *Ibid.,* pp. 77-78.

[Over all the races that lived in Anáhuac from the remotest cycles of traditional and hieroglyphic history, written in stone and revealed in the inviolable mystery of the temple, over all those primitive peoples adventurous and bold there hung from the first the sovereign legend of its prophecies.

It was the terror of the future. The formidable

While it is not possible to give here a resumé of the stories composing this group, some idea of their nature may be had from a summary of *La profecía de la catástrofe.* In it is told the story of a love affair between a captive maid of Tlaxcala and an Aztec warrior of high rank.

Mixtlexcatzín, an Aztec warrior, stole a beautiful captive maid from the house of the emperor, Moctecuhzoma, and fled with her at night across the lake. While slaves rowed the boat the two lovers abandoned themselves to voluptuous delights. In the moonlight they slept, rocked by gentle waves; and in their sleep the same vision appeared to both.

They dreamed that the city of Tenochtitlán had grown great and rich, that its priests kept the altars red with the blood of many captives, that captive women from the south made glad the great festivals with music and dancing. But

---

enigma of coming events that were to expand or annihilate the races, the burning and absolute undoing of its peoples, was ever before the rulers, the *tecuhtlis* and the priests of the Great Temple like the black, intangible, phantasmagoric and torrential descent of waters that from the high heavens fall, dragging down stars and plunging into the unfathomable depths whole nations with their triumphant kings and adored idols.]

a sense of impending doom made fitful this dream of glory. They heard from afar the roar of fierce warriors, while enormous eagles darkened the sky over Tenochtitlán. Netzahualcoyotl's prophecy was being fulfilled.

With the fair-skinned warriors were the *tigers* of Tlaxcala. Tenochtitlán, the great city of the Aztecs, was being consumed in red flames; but redder still were the tongues of fire of the strangers. The Mexican eagles circling over the city fell one by one into the fire until only the greatest eagle was left. But he too fell at last and Tenochtitlán was no more.

When the dreamers awoke, they had grown old. The delight of love had fled and there remained only the sad spirit of their dream that was soon to become reality.

Not only in this legend, but also in most of the stories composing this group, there is a vagueness reminiscent of some of the works of José Martí. Details are not drawn. Characters and moving forces are suggested in a few bold strokes and left to the reader's imagination, still veiled in half-light. Transitions in the stories leave wide gaps to be spanned; but at times the very atmosphere of vagueness becomes attractive.

Like many of the modernistic writers, Frías heightened the exotic element by the use of strange words of indefinite meaning. His use of omens reminds one dimly of Rubén Darío's *Heraldos,* but in Frías' work even death and destruction, unannounced by Darío, has her heralds. Some of Frías' beautiful maids from distant lands are, like Dario's Prince of Golconda or of China, mere vague creations of the author's fancy to give impression. Like Herrera y Reissig's "lilac preoccupations" disturbing the "illusions of the morning," Frías' subjective and psychic states colored the nature he painted.

The richness of description, dependent at times on unusual metaphors, that pervades much of this series of legends may be illustrated by the following quotations:

> Cantan las brisas de la tarde el himno del crepúsculo en las múltiples ramazones de los ahuehuetes melancólicos.[1]

> En torno del gran Tecpan de Texcotzingo extiéndese amplia y espesa maravillosísima guirnalda

---

[1]*Ibid.,* p. 83.

[The breezes of the evening sing the hymn of dusk among the branches of the melancholy *ahuehuetes.*]

de magníficos vergeles, soberbios mantos de
esmeralda cambiante, salpicada con manchas rojas,
como gotitas de sangre recién arrancada de la herida
de un colosal gigante . . .[1]

Tonoch, emperador de la luz, derrama con feroz
ansiedad de pasión sus caricias . . .[2]

. . . en la superabundancia perfumada y embriagante
de tan divinas selvas, detallaban relámpagos de plata
en las tibias noches al rayo de la luna o fúlgidas
centellas áureas en los breves crepúsculos, y tales
relámpagos argentinos, y tales fulguraciones de
oro Tonotich, los arrancaba de las líquidas láminas
de pequeños lagos . . . y de las serpientes mágicas
y eternamente cambiantes de los chorros y cascadas
blanquecinas, embellecidas por el príncipe dios del
fuego, al besar a su imposible amada, el agua.[3]

---

[1]*Ibid.*, pp. 83-84.

[Around the great Tecpan of Texcotzingo ex-
tends, wide and dense, a marvelous garland of magnificent flower gardens, superb mantles of shimmer-
ing emerald, sprinkled with red spots like little
drops of blood recently shed from the wound of a
colossal giant.]

[2]*Ibid.*, p. 84.

[Tonoch, Emperor of Light, sheds with the fierce
anxiety of passion his caresses . . .]

[3]*Ibid.*, p. 84.

[In the perfumed and intoxicating superabund-
ance of such divine forests, there flashed minute
gleams of silver on warm nights in the rays of the
moon or resplendent sparks of gold in the twilight,
and such silvery flashes, and such refulgence of
gold Tonotich drew from the liquid lamina of
little lakes . . . and from the magic eternally
changing serpents of the streams and whitish

¡Oh! lagunas tranquilas y dilatadas sobre cuyas
ondas ligeramente orladas de espuma, sobre las
márgenes floridas, las de las aguas azules que
devolvían al cielo el ósculo enorme y eterno del
Humeante Cíclope y la caricia intangible y
lánguida, melancólica, infinitamente tristísima de
la *Mujer Blanca*; ¡oh! vergeles radiosos que surgen
en la mente del evocador en un apoteósis épico y
tranquilo al mismo tiempo . . . la sombra augusta
del rey de Texcoco hubo de irradiar su grandeza
sobre vuestra hermosura . . . Fué el genio del hombre
proyectando su luz en la gran esplendidez muda de
las selvas.[1]

This series of stories is basically poetic in
conception. The haze of atmosphere of a strange
land of strange peoples, of unknown gods and
exotic animals that are messengers of heaven
and symbols of human traits blend with the

---

waterfalls, embellished by the divine prince of fire
on kissing his impossible lover, the water.]

[1]*Ibid.*, pp. 84-85.

[Oh! tranquil and far spread lagoons on whose
waves lightly specked with foam, on the flowered
banks, those of blue waters that returned to the
sky the enormous and eternal kiss of the *Smoking
Cyclops* and the intangible languid, melancholy
caress, infinitely sad, of the *White Woman*; oh!
radiant flower gardens that surge in the mind of
the dreamer in an apotheosis, epic and tranquil at
the same time . . . the august shadow of the king
of the Texoco was to radiate its grandeur over your
beauty . . . It was the genius of man projecting its
light into the great mute splendor of the forest.]

phantasy of physical nature to make harmonious interpretation that is more poetry than prose. The world presented here is no prosaic world with dissonant factors striving against each other, but a universe moving in harmony with destiny. Love with all of its beauty and life with all of its charm are but notes in the final chord of the gods.

¿Aguila o sol?, published in 1923, continues the series of studies of episodes of Mexican history as they affected the lives of the citizens of a small town. The author's interpretation of unrest in his country is most adequately expressed in a phrase he dropped in an inconspicuous place in his narrative, "the lyric idea of rebellion . . ."[1] The essentially epic nature of his people, as individuals and as a group, sought realization in defiance of authority.

> Mientras tengan
> licor las botellas
> bebamos en ellas
> hasta
> esperando
> que tal vez mañana
> clarín de campaña
> nos llame a pelear.[2]

---

[1] Heriberto Frías: *¿Aguila o sol?*, México, 1923, p. 231.
[2] *Ibid.*, p. 229.
    [While there is still

Revolution to the people was picturesque, colorful and stimulating. The heroine, fortunate in being betrothed to an industrious, intelligent, wealthy and peaceful boy while other girls of much higher social and financial standing than she were faced with permanent spinsterhood, dreamed of a man who had broken the law, who had been in prison, who had a reputation as a deceiver of women. She and other girls longed for a revolution that would make colorful heroes for them to love. She wanted violent passion, even though it were a flame that destroyed the basis of permanent happiness.

Into the mouth of the *gringo* and his son Frías put words of wisdom concerning Mexico's problems. These two wanted only the privilege of working in peace. Mr. Hanssen conceived of a new future for Mexico to be brought about by a new race formed by the intermarriage of

---

Liquor in the bottles
Let us drink from them

. . .

Hoping
That perhaps tomorrow,
The war bugle
Will call us to fight.]

Mexicans and more practical foreigners. The resulting union of colorful idealism and practicality would be the basis for a great civilization.

The story has an interesting plot, but, like many other Mexican historical novels, it contains long discussions of political movements and characters that have only a slight and indirect bearing on the plot. Some of those discussions make rather tedious reading.

The value of the work is in the author's interpretation of his own people and the forces involved in their social life. Their Quixotic hatred of injustice and their love of epic action and colorful individualism drew them inevitably into strife against the regime to which they were subject. One is left with the feeling that in Mexico no earthly regime would satisfy the people, that under the best of human government the *lyric idea of rebellion* would still assert itself.

The *Episodios militares mexicanos* is a collection of tales of the brave deeds of the national army during the fight for independence and the war with the United States. The author's intent was to glorify the Mexican heroes for the edification of Mexican youth. Patriotic sentiment leads him to such heights of loyalty that he sublimes all actions of the Mexican soldier; for example, with the stern righteousness of a Samuel looking to results in the remote future, he justified the savagery of the insurgent mobs in the sacking of Guanajuato, saying: "it was necessary . . . that fit of passion had to be tolerated." These men may have been cruel to one generation, but they were building for the ages to come by teaching humanity that sins against men's liberty must have a terrible retribution. There hangs over much of this work the atmosphere of glory of the sword of righteousness wielded by human hands under the inspiration of the gods of human liberty.

VICTORIANO SALADO ÁLVAREZ

Of the several series of historical episodes in novel form the best are those of Salado Álvarez. At times the style has the clearness, simplicity, and naturalness characteristic of Juan Valera. Like Valera, Salado Álvarez gives the impression that he is an unattached observer, quite unperturbed by noisy personal reaction. He is one of the few Mexican novelists capable of writing long narratives in the first person without self-consciousness. His almost philosophical calm and detachment from political partisan· ship and ephemeral literary schcols have so far appealed less than they should to a sensation-hunting public and to school-minded critics.

Though some Mexican authors can count a more impressive list of schools attended than Salado Álvarez, few show evidence of the cultural balance and poise discernible in his work. That poise and his refreshing freedom from the narrowness of artistic conception that characterizes the devotees of movements with narrow bases is traceable to his close acquaintance with the best of Spanish writers, especially those of the Golden Age. From them he learned the solid realism that is the best feature of his work.

In 1901 Salado Álvarez published a volume of stories under the title *De autos.* In 1902 he published in three volumes with a total of 1468 pages a long series of historical episodes which he called *De Santa Anna a la reforma.* In 1903 there appeared a second series of what he called *Episodios nacionales mexicanos* under the title *La intervención y el imperio,* in four volumes of 754, 737, 578, 713 pages respectively. In addition to these he wrote several short stories.

The series *De Santa Anna a la reforma* is superior to any series of Mexican historical episodes up to the time of its publication. In its truly fictional part it leaves little to be desired. It is a long story of the life of one Juan Pérez, told in the first person, with an immense amount of interpolated minutiae in the form of intimate glimpses of important political and literary characters of the period. In the collection of material for his work Salado Álvarez exhausted accessible periodicals of the period, and gleaned carefully the memoirs of acquaintances and little known books and documents, in search of human aspects of the period and its chief characters, attempting to bring to light fresh information instead of revamping the threadbare stories that constituted the patriotic equipment of various partisan groups and that had been the chief source of such writers as Juan A. Mateos. Salado Alvarez' work is therefore a study of human beings rather than of formal history, and yet through the human factors the basic conflict between the old regime and the reform movement becomes clear.

In the convincing story of the life of Juan Pérez from early childhood to advanced age, his contacts were with individuals that played various roles in the drama of the times, for no intelligent person, however low his rank, was without participation. But for Salado Álvarez those individuals did not lose their identity as such in the whirl of social forces; rather were those social forces outlined and made clear by the study of intimate reaction.

In keeping with this attitude the author consistently left the analysis of the period to his characters rather than resort to formal dissertation. The heated debates that raged between them, the expression of their personal opinions and intimate feelings are the devices the author used to describe the forces at work. Attack and defense, abuse and justification, loyalties and opposition are all a part of the writer's scheme of delineation; but it is the character that speaks and the writer that records. At times it seems that the author is permitting each side to analyze its opponent with unerring accuracy, being convinced that only when each is appraising itself is its judgment poor.

But for all the author's detachment and calmness, the severity of the struggle of attitudes and the resulting destruction is impressive. The conservative cries, "Long live religion; down with tolerance" and "Religion and *fueros*" are answered by the liberals' determination to destroy every vestige of the past. It is clear that in many instances both sides are making dramatic phrases to cover selfish interests. In the struggle the position of the moderate liberals stand out as the only basically sound one.

The work *De Santa Anna a la reforma* attempts to give an understanding of almost every phase of Mexican life during that period. Frequent comments on literary developments are linked with the plot in such a manner as not to seem out of place, as may be seen by an examination of chapter VIII of volume II. In a judicious criticism of the novels of the epoch the author wrote:

> Las novelas eran todas fúnebres y sentimentales. Ante todo había que ser *exquisito, delicado*. De un poeta se decía que su paso era tan tenue que no se sentía, que era incorpóreo, que era intangible, que no hollaba la tierra. Para alabar a una niña, el piropo más fino era llamarla *sensible* . . . En los libros se huía cuidosamente de tratar cosa del país, juzgándose quizá que no eran dignas del coturno. Fernando Orozco escribió una deliciosa, admirable, potentísima novela y apenas se llega a saber donde

acontecen los sucesos de ella. Juan Díaz, Castillo
y sobre todo Prieto creían que algo explotable
podía haber aquí y escribían de asuntos nacionales;
pero poco gustaban esas cosas . . .[1]

Of poetry of the epoch Salado Álvarez remarked:

. . leyeron más versos. ¿Quiénes? Todo el mundo,
todos los que sabían leer, porque en aquellos benditos
tiempos no había regocijo, duelo, acto civil o
religioso que no se acompañara con versos, cojos
ellos y maltrechos, pero versos al fin.[2]

---

[1] V. Salado Álvarez: *De Santa Anna a la reforma,
memorias de un veterano,* México, 1902-1903, Vol. II,
p. 90.

[The novels were all sad and sentimental. Above
everything a work had to be *exquisite, delicate.*
Of one poet it was said that his step was so delicate
that it could not be heard, that he was incorporeal,
that he was intangible, that he did not step on the
earth. In order to praise a young lady the best com-
pliment was to call her *of delicate sensibility . . .*
In books writers carefully avoided dealing with
things of our country, thinking perhaps that they
were not worthy. Fernando Orozco wrote a de-
licious, admirable and powerful novel and scarcely
can one determine where its events took place. Juan
Díaz, Castillo and above all Prieto believed that
there was something of value in this country and so
they wrote about national events, but those things
created little interest.]

[2] *Ibid.,* p. 53.

[. . . they read more poetry. Who? Everybody, all
who knew how to read because in those blessed
times there was no rejoicing, grief, civil or relig-

On another occasion he wrote:

> . . . no se puede escribir de aquellos tiempos sin hablar de lo que entonces llamábamos *el lenguaje de las musas*. Se vivía en verso . . .[1]

And again:

> Nada nos importaba la Academia ni el perro judío que la había inventado, pues a fuer de ciudadanos de una nación libre, pensábamos no había que hacer maldito el caso de los dictados de una corporación extranjera y por añadidura monárquica y archicatólica.[2]

Education was described as follows:

> . . . las escuelas son atrasadísimas, y que de nuestros seminarios apenas salen discutidores, pero no gentes de ciencia ni piedad; que no hay en todos nuestros colegios cátedras de hebreo ni de idiomas modernos, ni de historia profana, ni de nada, en fin, de acuerdo con las luces del siglo; y que toda esa gente que se mantiene a expensas de los conventos es una turba de haraganes que, como tiene segura la comida,

---

ious act that was not accompanied with verses, lame and malformed, but verses after all.]

[1]*Ibid.*, p. 87.

[. . . one can not write of those times without speaking of what we then called *the language of the Muses*. Everybody lived in poetry.]

[2]*Ibid.*, p. 90.

[We did not care a fig for the Academy nor the dog of a Jew that invented it, for by virtue of citizenship in a free nation, we thought we did not have to pay any attention to the dictates of a corporation, foreign and in addition monarchial and arch-Catholic.]

se dedica a vivir de holgazana o a hacer picardías de todas clases.[1]

The political corruption and turmoil that characterized Mexican affairs of the times are effectively set forth in frequent statements like the following:

Como aquí todo se ha arreglado con planes y pronunciamientos; como en aquellos . . . tiempos cada politicastro se figuraba tener el secreto de la salvación del país, mediante un documento en que se ordenara a los mexicanos ser justos y felices, a cada parada de la diligencia teníamos un comisionado que llegaba reventando caballos para proponer . . .[2]

---

[1]*Ibid.,* Vol. I, p. 32.

[. . . the schools are very backward and from our seminaries there come out only talkers, but not people of learning or piety; for there are not in any of our schools chairs of Hebrew nor of modern languages, nor of secular history, nor of anything, in fact, in keeping with the developments of the century; and all that group of people which is supported at the expense of the convent is a band of loafers who since they are assured of a livelihood, dedicate themselves to idleness and to roguery of all classes.]

[2]*Ibid.,* p. 133.

[Just as in this period everything has been arranged by plan and decrees, in that day and time every petty politician thought he had the secret of the salvation of the country wrapped up in a document in which Mexicans were commanded to be just and happy; with each stop of the stage coach

Don Antonio Haro regó mucha plata entre los jefes; pero, si te vi no me acuerdo; la cogían, la embolsaban y *pax Cristi*. Bribón de aquellos hubo que se pronunciara tres o cuatro veces con su gente, sin perjuicio de despronunciarse sin ellas otras tantas.[1]

With unerring accuracy the author sought out the weaknesses of his country and its people. Concerning Mexicans he wrote the following eloquent summary:

. . . aquella gente hecha a estimar las palabras más que el contenido . . .[2]

There are passages in this novel that remind one of Manuel Payno's pictures in *Los bandidos de Río Frío*. The following description of Mexico City will suffice to show this trend:

A poco entramos en unas callejuelas torcidas con casucas insignificantes, habitadas por viejas sucias,

---

we had a commissioner who traveled hurriedly making proclamations . . .]

[1]*Ibid.*, p. 115.

[Don Antonio Haro lavished bribes upon the leaders; but "if I ever saw you, I don't remember"; the leaders took the bribes, pocketed them and *pax Cristi*. There was a rascal among them who with his followers rebelled three or four times, without binding himself not to about face without his followers whenever he pleased.]

[2]*Ibid.*, p. 178.

[. . . that people inclined to value words more than the content of those words.]

muchachos mugrosos y léperos borrachos. Iba el
coche deshaciendo los montones de basura, atascán-
dose en los baches del camino, bordeando las atarjeas,
ahuyentando a los perros que se solazaban en el
cadáver de cualquier animal muerto. Avanzó más
espacio y me sorprendieron casas más altas que las
que estaba acostumbrado a ver en Guadalajara, pero
tan tristes, tan faltas de color y de vida, que me
asombré de que un cielo tan hermoso abrigara tan
mezquino paisaje; estábamos en la ciudad de Mexico.[1]

While there is nothing deep nor profoundly
psychological in the works of this author, he
is one of Mexico's best stylists. He differs from
Altamirano in that he is moderate, clear and
simple in expression while the latter's prose is
many times sufficiently adorned to approach
the tone of poetry. There is more color and lyric

---

[1]*Ibid.*, pp. 137-138.

[A little later we entered some crooked little
streets with insignificant hovels, inhabited by dirty
old women, grimy little boys, and drunken
wretches. The coach went plowing through piles of
filth, getting stuck in the mud holes of the road,
going around the drain pipes, scattering the dogs
that were stuffing themselves on the carcass of a
dead animal. It went ahead and I was surprised at
the houses, which were taller than those I was accustomed to see in Guadalajara, but so unattractive,
so devoid of color and life that I wondered how so
beautiful a sky could cover such a sorry scene; we
were in the city of Mexico.]

beauty in Altamirano, but more simplicity in Salado Álvarez.

Rodríguez Beltrán was born in Tlacotalpam, Vera Cruz, September 24, 1866. Actively engaged at various times in the fields of journalism, business, and teaching, he made good use of an unusual mental ability and opportunity for self-directed study. His most important position was that of director of the secondary schools of Jalapa in which he occupied the chair of literature.

But whatever his occupation, Rodríguez Beltrán's interest has been in literature. From that interest he reaped not so much non-functional encyclopedic knowledge of the important compositions of famous writers of many countries, as was the case with many Mexican writers, but a critical judgment and good taste that place him among Mexico's best stylists. The fact that his *Pajarito* had only one edition, while works of such writers as Juan A. Mateos and Riva Palacio had many is entirely insignificant in the appraisal of his compositions, for such popularity depends on public taste.

The only novel of Rodríguez Beltrán with which we are concerned here is *Pajarito,* and there is some reason for ruling it out of the class of historical novels. The characters are not historical; in fact, the only historical factor involved is the work's general setting in the period immediately after the fall of Maximilian, and very little would have been lost if any other comparatively recent period had been chosen. But the spirit of that epoch is prominent enough in parts of the work to justify the inclusion of this novel in the historical group.

The most interesting manifestation of the state of mind of the people of Mexico in that decade of Mexican history is found in the description of children's games. The author pictures little boys engrossed in military games, marching, executing numerous maneuvers, improvising bugles and drums, firing on imaginary enemies with sticks used as guns, using recesses during school hours for the development of defense and attack strategy. Anxious to devote as much time as possible to their pretended battles, the youngsters would rise early in the mornings and go into the streets sounding through cupped hands an imitation of reveille bugle call. They marched about their chores with military step, carrying broomsticks on their shoulders as guns. Indeed, in few novels have the emotional preoccupations of a generation been shown so well by an analysis of the attitudes of children. A fair novel in general characteristics, *Pajarito* is unusually attractive in this regard.

Unfortunately, however, the selection of material was not guided by rigid demands for unity. Starting out with a plan that called for detailed study of the reactions of individuals in a given environment and a graphic description of background, the author seemed to lose the courage or the industry necessary to carry out his initial intentions, and compromised with the traditional insistence on a thrilling narrative. After he began to occupy himself with the intrigues for the fortune of Illescas, the story lost heavily in literary value; and thereafter, only when he returned occasionally to the simple folk of the village and their ways did he maintain even a passable level of interest. In spite of the lapses into sensational plot in some parts of the narrative, however, the description of the manner of life of the humble classes of Mexico is done in

such fashion that the characters appear natural.
Their speech, their virtues and vices, their in-
continence, their hard labors for a miserable
existence, their loyalties, the paucity of their
education and their personal attitudes are so
realistically recorded that they live and breathe
in the pages of the book.

The juvenile characters, especially Chencho
and Pajarito, seem of actual flesh and bone.
Nicho's experiences from pre-school age to maturity are truly those of a little boy thrown into
cruelly difficult situations of life. His childish
realization that his origin was in some way irregular; his bewilderment at the fact that he had
no father as other boys did; his attachment to
the heroic woman he called mother, and his
sorrow for the hard lot that had fallen to her in
life; his fear of school and all other experiences
in which she did not share; the complete domination of his spirit by his teacher and playmates
at school; his gradual identification of himself
with the gang of *arribeños,* one of the gangs
of boys; the expansion of his personality
brought about by the recognition on the part of
his companions of his superiority in climbing
trees, an ability that won for him the nickname

"Pajarito"; his exhaustion from hard labor as an apprentice in the service of masons and carpenters, and his pride when for the first time he put into his mother's hands his week's wages —these and numerous other experiences seem real indeed.

Almost as interesting as his description of individual boys is the author's account of the activities of the two gangs of boys, the *arribeños* and the *abajeños*. Serious sociological studies of this gang spirit among boys have been written with less accuracy than Rodríguez Beltrán's. That the two groups became convenient media for the expression of the years of struggle against a foreign invader was entirely natural. Nothing is more plausible than that each gang commanded by its leader should drill incessantly for set sham battles between the two.

An idea of the author's sympathetic portrayal of the spirit of boys as well as his description of background may be had from the following picture of youngsters returning home after a day spent in the woods instead of at school where their parents thought they were:

—Mucho que la hemo gozao; pero falta ora lo pior . . .¿ y con qué salimo pa que no noj peguen?—

Todos dieron la callada por respuesta, para

ponerse a pensar en la manera de preparar el embuste que les evitaría el castigo.

Pajarito, quizás fuera el que más se arrepentía de la escapatoria, y aquella pasajera alegría que alborotó un instante su natural y taciturna tristeza de huérfano y desgraciado hijo, tornóse en honda y pertinaz melancolía.

Venían cabizbajos, pensativos, uno detrás de otro por las sendas angostas; esquivando el lodo de los barriales y salvando el agua cenagosa de los pantanos.

Chencho, por darse ánimo, silbaba, y Palitos, para acompañarlo canturreaba desafinadamente.

La noche se venía encima con su cortejo de sombras y su solemnidad de silencios; el antes vistoso y esplendente paisaje se esfumaba, se perdía en un cendal de sombras macizas y de umbrías calladas; los trabajadores pasaban para sus cabañas con el machete al hombro y pendiente de la cacha el tenate del bastimento, el cual tenate traía por único contenido la esbelta y vacía botella en que se llevó el aguardiente para reanimarse en las duras tareas de labriego.

Los rapaces corrían y tiraban al camino los cañutos de caña que eran estorbo para la marcha acelerada; las copas de los árboles se confundían a distancia con la negrura de los cielos, y sólo los troncos se enfilaban y sucedían como dispersos y firmes centinelas del boscaje . . .[1]

---

[1]Cayetano Rodríguez Beltrán: *Pajarito,* México, 1908, pp. 178-180.

[—We have sure had a good time; but the worst part is yet to come . . . and how are we going to get out of a licking?—

They were all silent, thinking how they could

Another noteworthy feature of *Pajarito* is the
type of tragedy that maintains itself consistent-

---

best prepare a lie that would let them escape punishment.

Pajarito perhaps was the one who felt most remorse over the escapade; and that temporary joy
that displaced for an instant his natural and uncom-
municative sadness, born of his state as an orphan
and as an unfortunate child, was turned into a deep
and persistent melancholy.

They were returning crestfallen, thoughtful, one
behind the other in the narrow paths; avoiding the
mud of the holes and jumping the dirty water of
the swampy places.

Chencho, in order to give himself courage,
whistled as he went, and Palitos, in order to keep
him company, hummed out of tune.

Night was coming on with its cortege of shadows
and its silent solemnity; the landscape which a
little while before had been colorful and splendid
was becoming smoky; it was becoming lost behind
a gauze of heavy shadows and of silent groves; the
laborers were making their way to their cabins
with their machetes slung over their shoulders and
hanging from the handles, their dinner pails emptied
of all contents save dry bottles in which they had
carried whiskey with which to console themselves
in their hard labor.

The mischievous truants ran and threw down in
the road the joints of cane which had become a hindrance in their hastened march; the tops of the
trees became confused in the distance with the darkness of the skyline, and only the trunks of the
trees stood out in a row like scattered and motion-
less sentinels of the forest.]

ly above superficial sentimentality. Rodríguez
Beltrán created no sniveling types, even in the
most trying situation. His tearless men, women
and children appear as silent victims of dry,
cutting sorrow, too deep to bring forth floods
of weeping and too paralyzing to be vocal.
Whatever of weeping there is, is done off stage.
Pajarito, after being taunted by the Regidor's
son with the fact that he has no father is described as follows:

> . . . de camino para su casa iba pensativo, doliente,
> y humillado; fueron como una brusca y brutal
> revelación las palabras hirientes del hijo del Regidor;
> ahora le salían al rostro la pena que de años atrás
> traía dentro, muy dentro, lacerante y oculta,
> traidora y tenaz, sin saber qué era aquello que le
> anudaba la garganta y le humedecía los ojos; . . .
> Y se le agolpaban . . . ya en tropel, ya confusos, ya
> claros, todos los días infortunados de su niñez
> desvalida y pobre; pasaban en desfile doloroso las
> velas largas y los trabajos duros de su madre triste,
> austera y hasta huraña; . . .[1]

[1]*Ibid.*, pp. 192-193.

[. . . along the road to his house he went thoughtful, deeply hurt and depressed; the cutting words of
the Alderman's son had been an abrupt and cruel
revelation; and now there came out in his little face
the pain that for years he had carried somewhere
inside, deep inside, lacerating and hidden, treach-
erous and tenacious, without understanding what
it was that hurt in his throat and made his eyes

Rodríguez sensed, as does every good tragedian, that grief that gives itself to copious, boisterous weeping and complaint is not good tragedy; that the most convincing tragedy reveals pain and grief borne in comparative silence; that the measure of true tragedy is the degree to which the author makes the reader conscious of the restraint imposed by the characters on the expression of their sorrow; in short, that good tragedy is found only in a sense of restrained grief, in hidden grief, in silent suffering. Other writers of more universal fame than Rodríguez Beltrán are much inferior to him in this regard; certainly his understanding of this phase of literary art is rare in Mexican literature.

Though landscape painting is not prominent in *Pajarito*, there are some excellent descriptive passages. The view of the fields and woods surrounding the village as seen from the church tower[1] and that of the countryside[2] through

fill with tears. And there filed before him . . . now in a group, now confused, now clear, all those unfortunate days of his childhood, full of loneliness and poverty; there passed in a sad parade the long vigil and the hard work of his sad mother, austere and even shy.]

[1]*Ibid.*, pp. 103-111.

[2]*Ibid.*, Chap. x, especially pp. 158-159.

which the boys passed on one of their excursions are especially well done.

The work has some weaknesses. That part of the story that presents the wealthy old man suddenly concerned over the welfare of his illegitimate son in whom he had manifested no interest until the boy reached maturity, whom, in fact, he had never seen and whose mother he had permitted to die of overwork, detracts from the effectiveness of the novel. It is not plausible that the old man would advertise far and wide for information concerning his son and not think of going personally to the town where he knew the mother originally lived and where she and her son had continued to live without interruption. Any child in that village could have given him the information he wanted. Neither is it easy to believe that a man of Illesca's understanding of human nature would be so easily duped by his nephew's crude schemes to keep him from finding his son.

MARCELINO DÁVALOS

Marcelino Dávalos is the author of a group of ten stories dealing with the victims of the Díaz regime living as exiles and slaves in Yucatan. There were two editions of the entire collection, one in 1915 and the second in 1916. The 1915 edition carries the following statement: "Suscritos en Chan Santa Cruz, Q. R., 1902 a 1908."

The stories are rather well unified by the role of the author as eye-witness of different aspects of the same abuse, and by the constant presence of the political machine as the instrument of obstruction.

Dávalos makes literary material of the tyranny of Diaz' rule. In some of his stories the various governmental agencies, including the judiciary, appear as instruments of political expediency and favoritism that destroyed the most elemental rights of men. The main characters are, as a rule, honorable men sent to Yucatan, made to endure suffering comparable to that of ancient galley slaves, driven to despair by the gang drivers and wrecked in health by malaria and starvation, merely because their presence at home interfered with the designs of individuals with political connections. One man's farm was coveted by a political boss; another man's wife was desired by a friend of the local judge; a group of men demanded a living wage of a great corporation—all of them were sent to Yucatan without trial. Those who made trouble for the dominant regime were conscripted into the army and transported to Yucatan to live the life of slaves. Especially liable to such treatment were industrial workers who complained about being paid their meager wages in script redeemable only at company-owned stores where prices were exhorbitant.

The style is direct, simple and unadorned; in forceful, almost elliptical manner the author expresses his reaction. The economy of language is severe at times. There is none of the artificiality of sentiment and manipulated episode so common in the nineteenth century.

There are evident traces of naturalism in *Carne de cañon*. The disintegration of the character of Anita, a virtuous wife who followed her husband to Yucatan in spite of his protests and the hardships she foresaw, is clearly the result of the influence of the naturalistic movement. In the vicious whirl of degradation and injustice, she became a moral derelict, weeping at each step, "I do not understand it!" There is also a note of pessimistic determinism in this lack of will and in the impossibility of self-determination.

The author's pictures of the injustices of the times seem overdrawn; but their accuracy is attested to by John Kenneth Miller in his *Barbarous Mexico*. Whatever be the reader's opinion of the authenticity of Miller's account and of Dávalos' depiction, it is significant that two writers should give so nearly the same version without consultation.

There is in Dávalos' work considerable emphasis on the biological basis of human attitudes and reactions. This emphasis at times suggests Pío Baroja.

Just as Mateos was the apologist of the revolution and of the reform movement, so Dávalos was the scourge of tyranny in the Díaz regime.

V

CONCLUSION

Though a chronological order is probably the best available for the presentation of materials involved in such a study as this, it has the disadvantage of failing to provide basic unity and synthesis. It is the purpose of this conclusion to remedy this defect.

In the preface the reader's attention was called to certain trends in the Mexican historical novel. He may now consider more fully in retrospect those same trends along with other critical conclusions.

It is quite significant that among the writers of historical novels in Mexico there is not one of importance whose interpretation is not rooted in social liberalism. One seeks in vain among them a writer of absolutist or even of highly conservative convictions. They are unanimous in the use of authoritarianism as the one factor that destroys human happiness and frustrates human aspirations. Tyranny and oppression from the time of Montezuma to that of Porfirio Díaz are the evil forces of dissolution and ruin, and freedom is the goddess of beauty. There are few novels that have as their source of interest the archeological appeal of Walter Scott's works and those of his followers. Mexican historical novelists found little of the picturesque and of archaic flavor between the coming of Cortés and the revolt of Hidalgo. Their art was severely righteous in its preoccupation with justice and liberty. Its creative power was generally applied to fashioning monsters of injustice and saints of freedom.

Such a liberal emphasis contrasts rather sharply with the traditional emphasis of much of European romanticism, and explains the fact that Erckmann-Chatrian made a deeper impression on Mexican historical novelists than did Walter Scott.

As was pointed out in the preface, the historical novels of Mexico can be divided into two groups, the romantic historical novels and those of contemporary history. The former sought their material in the pre-conquest, the conquest and the colonial epoch, just as Europe had returned to its middle ages for materials; the latter dealt with historical events that were, broadly speaking, contemporary. But the treatment accorded the materials of both groups was conventional, with patriotism and loyalty to liberalism as the principal emotive force, and with an ever-present tendency to sublimate the representatives of freedom.

The most important novels that belong to the romantic historical group are the anonymous *Jicoténcal,* Justo Sierra's *La hija del judío,* most of the historical novels of Eligio Ancona and of Riva Palacio, Pascual Almazán's *Un hereje y un musulmán, Amor y suplicio* and *Doña Marina* of Ireneo Paz, and the *Leyendas históricas mexicanas* of Heriberto Frías.

To the group of novels of contemporary history belong Manuel Payno's *El fistol del diablo, Los bandidos de Río Frío* and several of his short historical stories, Díaz Covarrubia's *Gil Gómez el insurgente, o la hija del médico,* Altamirano's *Clemencia,* the long series of *Episodios nacionales mexicanos* of Olavarría y Ferrari, nearly all of the novels of Juan A. Mateos, Ireneo Paz' *Leyendas históricas, Eva* of Martínez de Castro, practically all the works of Heriberto Frías except his *Leyendas históricas mexicanas,* the long series of episodes of Salado Álvarez that were published under the two titles *De Santa Anna a la Reforma* and *La intervención y el Imperio, Pajarito* of Rodríguez Beltrán and *Carne de cañon* of Marcelino Dávalos.

In the matter of inspiration and native artistic capacity Mexican historical novelists as a whole were not lacking. They were keenly aware of their role in the trying ordeal through which their country was passing in its struggle to constitute itself a nation on an idealistic basis, and their judgment of ultimate human values and their evaluation of human experience are worthy of praise. But in the matter of literary form can be seen evidences of lack of experience and discipline. Such a weakness, however, was inherent in the social and artistic youth of the nation. In short, their defect was not one of vision, but of form.

BIBLIOGRAPHY

CRITICAL AND BIBLIOGRAPHICAL WORKS

Abreu y Gómez, Ermilo: *Justo Sierra O'Reilly y la novela*, in *Contemporáneos*, México, no. 35, April, 1931, pp. 39-73.

Agüeros, V.: *Nuestra literatura*, in his *Obras literarias, Biblioteca de Autores Mexicanos*, Vol. VIII, México, 1897.

Altamirano, Ignacio Manuel: *Florencio del Castillo*, in *El Renacimiento*, México, Vol. I, 1869, pp. 500-502; also p. 90.

————— *Revistas literarias de México*, México, Imp. de T. F. Neve, 1868.

Blanco Fombona, Rufino: *Letras y letrados de Hispano-América*, París, 1908.

Coester, A.: *The Literary History of Spanish America*, New York, 1921.

Daireaux, M.: *Panorama de la Littérature Hispano-Américaine*, Paris, 1930.

Darío, Rubén: *España contemporánea*, París, 1901.

Fairchild, H. N.: *The Noble Savage, a Study in Romantic Naturalism*, Columbia University Press, 1928.

Gamboa, Federico: *La novela mexicana*, México, Gómez de la Puente, 1914.

González Obregón, Luis: *Breve noticia de los novelistas mexicanos en el siglo xix*, México, 1889.

———— *Noticia biográfica*, in *Biblioteca de Autores Mexicanos*, Vol. XXI, pp. v-xv.

González Peña, Carlos: *Historia de la literatura mexicana*, México, Sec. de Educación Pública, 1928.

Hurtado y Palencia: *Historia de la literatura española*, Madrid, 1925.

Iguíniz, Juan B.: *Bibliografía de Novelistas Mexicanos, Monografías bibliográficas mexicanas*, México, 1926.

Jiménez Rueda, Julio: *Historia de la literatura mexicana*, México, Editorial Cultura, 1928.

Lafragua, José María: *Literatura*, in *Ensayo literario, colección de composiciones sobre bellas letras, ciencias y artes*, Puebla, 1838, pp. 49-50.

Leonard, Irving A.: *A Great Savant of Seventeenth Century Mexico: Carlos Siguenza y Góngora*, in *Hispania*, Vol. X, 1927, No. 6, pp. 399-408.

———— *Romances of Chivalry in the Spanish Indies*, in *Modern Philology, Publications of the University of California*, Vol. XVI, No. 3, pp. 219 *et seq.*

López Portillo y Rojas, José: *La novela. Breve ensayo*, México, Tip. Vizcaíno y Viamonte, 1906.

Maigron, L.: *Le Roman historique a l'époque romantique*, Paris, 1912.

Mazatlán Literario, Mazatlán, 1889.

Medina, José Toribio: *La imprenta en México*, Santiago de Chile, 1909.

Meléndez, Concha: *Novelas históricas de México*, in *El Libro y el Pueblo*, México, Vol. XIII, No. 3, November, 1935, pp. 113-124.

Moreno Cora, Silvestre: *La crítica literaria en México*, Orizaba, Vera Cruz, 1907.

Olavarría y Ferrari, Enrique: *El arte literaria en México*, 2nd edition, Madrid, Espinosa y Bautista, n. d., probably 1878.

Palau y Dulcet: *Manual del librero hispanoamericano*, Barcelona, 1923-1927, tomo cuarto.

Pimentel, Francisco: *Obras completas*, México, Tip. Económica, 1903-1904, Vol. V.

Piñeyro, Enrique: *El romanticismo en España,* París, n. d.

El Renacimiento, México, 1869, Vol. I.

Riva Palacio, Vicente: *Los ceros. Galería de contemporáneos,* México, Imp. de F. Díaz de León, 1882.

Santacilia, Pedro: *Del movimiento literario en México,* México, Imp. del gobierno, 1868.

Spell, J. R.: *The Literary Works of Manuel Payno,* in *Hispania,* Vol. XII, 1929, pp. 347-356.

Torres Rioseco, Arturo: *Bibliografía de la novela mexicana,* Cambridge, Mass., Harvard University Press, 1933.

Ugarte, M.: *La joven literatura hispanoamericana,* París, 1915.

Urbina, Luis G.: *La vida literaria de México,* Madrid, Sánchez Hnos., 1917.

SOURCES OF BACKGROUND MATERIAL

Agras, Jesús: *Reflecciones sobre la naturaleza y origen de los males y trastornos que han producido la decadencia de México,* Guadalajara, Tip. de la Agencia General, etc., 1864.

Alamán, Lucas: *Historia de México*, México, Imp. de J. M. Lara, 1849-1852. 5 Vols.

Altamirano, Ignacio Manuel: *Paisajes y leyendas*, México, Imp. y lit. esp., 1884.

Alva Ixtlilxóchitl, Fernando de: *Historia chichimeca*, México, Oficina tip. de la Secretaría de Fomento, 1891-1892. 2 Vols.

Alvarado Tezozomoc, Hernando de: *Crónica mexicana*, México, Imp. y lit. de I. Paz, 1878.

Ancona, Eligio: *Historia de Yucatán*, Barcelona, Imp. de J. Jesús, 1889-1905, especially Vol. III, libro sexto.

Arroniz, Joaquín: *Ensayo de una historia de Orizaba*, Orizaba, Imp. de J. B. Aburto, 1867.

El Ateneo Mexicano, México, Imp. de V. G. Torres, tomo I, 1844.

Autos de fe en México, for the years 1646, 1647, 1648, 1649 and 1659. The first two published by Imp. de Francisco Robledo, 1646 and 1647 respectively, the third by Juan Ruiz, 1648, and fourth by Antonio Calderón, 1649, and the fifth by Vda. de B. Calderón, 1659. All these printers were official printers for the *Santo Oficio.*

Bancroft, Hubert Howe: *History of Mexico,* Vols. IV and V, San Francisco, Cal., 1885 and 1887 respectively.

Barreiro, Lic. M.: *El porvenir de Yucatán y ligera ojeada sobre su situación actual,* Mérida, 1864.

Bazaine, Francois A.: *Minute des despeches,* March 24, 1864, in *Correspondencia de Bazaine,* Vol. VI, p. 1012, (García Library).

Bustamante, Carlos María: *Campañas de Calleja,* México, Imp. del Águila, 1828.

——— *Cuadro histórico,* México, Imp. de J. M. Lara, 1843-1846.

Callcott, Wilfrid Hardy: *Church and State in Mexico,* Durham, N. C., Duke University Press, 1926.

Casas, Bartolomé de las: *Breve relación de la destrucción de las Indias,* Philadelphia, 1821.

——— *Historia de las Indias,* edited by José María Vigil, México, I. Paz, 1877.

Castellanos, Juan de: *Elegías de varones ilustres*

de Indias, in *Biblioteca de Autores Españoles,* Madrid, Imp. de la Publicidad, 1850, Vol. IV.

Castillo Negrete, Emilio: *México en el siglo xx,* México, 1875, especially Vol. I.

Cavo, Andrés: *Los tres siglos de México durante el gobierno español,* México, L. Abadiano y Valdés, 1836-1838. 4 Vols.

Chapman, Charles Edward: *Colonial Hispanic America: A History,* Macmillan, New York, 1923.

Códice Ramírez, México, Imp. y lit. de I. Paz, 1878.

Colección de libros raros y curiosos que tratan de América, Madrid, 1891-1902.

Corti, Egon Caesar: *Maximilian and Charlotte of Mexico,* New York and London, Alfred A. Knopf, 1929. 2 Vols.

Diario de México, México, Vol. XIII, 1810.

Díaz del Castillo, Bernal: *The Discovery and Conquest of Mexico, edited from the only exact copy of the original manuscript by Genaro García,* translated by A. P. Maudsley, New York and London, Harper Bros., 1928.

Ercilla, Alonso de: *La Araucana*, Madrid, Imp. Nacional, 1866.

Gaceta de México, México, 1810, Vol. II, and 1812, Vol. III.

García, Genaro and Pereyra, Carlos: *Documentos ineditos o muy raros para la historia de México*, México, 1906, Vol. V.

Gruening, E. H.: *Mexico and its Heritage*, New York, Century Co., 1928.

Hernández y Dávalos, Juan E.: *Colección de documentos*, México, J. M. Sandoval, 1877-1882.

Instrucciones que los virreyes de Nueva España dejaron a sus sucesores, México, 1867.

Lerdo de Tejada, Miguel: *Cuadro sinóptico de la República Mexicana en 1856*, México, I. Cumplido, 1856.

Liceo Mexicano, México, J. M. Lara, 1844, Vols. I and II.

López, Vicente Fidel: *La novia del hereje o la Inquisción de Lima*, Buenos Aires, 1917. (Argentine novel).

Lovalle, Francois: *Etudes historiques sur le Méxique au point de vue politique et social, d'apres des documents originaux mexicains*, Paris, 1856.

Mayer, Brantz: *Mexico as it was and as it is*, New York, New World Press, 1844.

―――― *Mexico, Aztec, Spanish and Republican*, Hartford, S. Drake and Co., 1851. 2 Vols.

Mecham, J. Lloyd: *Church and State in Latin America*, Chapel Hill, University of North Carolina Press, 1934.

México como nación independiente, descripción de su estado moral, político, intelectual, etc., artículo traducido del periódico literario Revista Trimestre de Filadelfia, Dec., 1827, México, 1828.

Mora, José M. L.: *México y sus revoluciones*, París, Lib. de Rosa, 1836.

El Museo Mexicano, México, 1843-1845, Vols. II, III and IV.

Negrete, Emilio del: *México en el siglo xx*, México, 1875.

Ortega, José de: *Historia del Nayarit, Sonora, Sinaloa y ambas Californias*, México, Tip. de Abadiano, 1887.

Palma, Ricardo: *Los anales de la Inquisción de Lima*, Madrid, Tip. de Ricardo Fe, 1897.

Pastor, A. R.: *The Chivalry and Military Orders of Spain*, in Prestage, Edgar: *Chivalry*, New York, Knopf, 1928, pp. 109-140.

Pérez Gallardo: *Diario de las operaciones y movimientos del ejército federal hasta su entrada a la capital de la República*, México, I. Cumplido, 1861.

Pérez Hernández: *Estadística de la República Mexicana*, Guadalajara, 1862.

Poinsett, J. R.: Letter dated March 10, 1829, to the American Secretary of State, in *Collection of Correspondence of American Ambassadors* compiled by Justin H. Smith, Vol. II, pp. 317-338. (In García library).

Ramírez, Ignacio M.: *Obras*, México, 1889.

Recopilación de leyes de Indias, 1681 edition, Libro I, título x, leyes vi, vii, viii, and título xxiv, ley iv.

Report of the Committee for the study of Educational Conditions in Mexico, Cincinnati, 1916.

Revista Mexicana, México, I. Cumplido, 1835.

Riva Palacio, Vicente: *México a través de los siglos*, Barcelona, 1889.

Rivera Cambas, Manuel: *Los gobernantes de*

México, México, Imp. de J. M. Aguilar Ortiz, 1872-1873.

Robertson, William Spence: *History of the Latin-American Nations*, D. Appleton and Co., 1912.

La Semana de las Señoritas, México, Imp. de Juan R. Navarro, 1851-1852. 5 Vols.

Semanario de las Señoritas Mexicanas, México, Imp. de Vicente G. Torres, 1841-1842, Vols. I, II and III.

Stevenson, W. B.: *Twenty Years Residence in South America*, London, 1829.

Tornel y Mendíbil: *Breve reseña histórica*, México, Imp. de Cumplido, 1852.

Varios documentos sobre la Inquisición en México, compiled by Genaro García. (In García library).

Historiadores primitivos de Indias, edited by Enrique de Vedia, in *Biblioteca de Autores Españoles*, Madrid, Vols. XXII and XXVI.

Walton: *Exposé on the Dissentions of Spanish America*, London, 1814.

Ward, H. G.: *Mexico in 1827*, London, 1828.

Zavala, Lorenzo de: *Ensayo histórico de las revoluciones de México desde 1808 hasta 1830*, París, Imp. de P. Dupont, 1831-1832.

Zerecero, Anastasio: *Memorias para la historia de las revoluciones de México*, México, Imp. del Gobierno, 1869.

NOVELS

Almazán, Pascual: *Un hereje y un musulmán*, México, 1870.

Altamirano, Ignacio Manuel: *Clemencia*, 3rd edition, México, 1880.

Ancona, Eligio: *La cruz y la espada*, París, Lib. de Rosa y Bouret, 1866. 2 Vols.

———— *El filibustero*, París, Lib. de Rosa y Bouret, 1866. 2 Vols.

———— *Los mártires del Anáhuac*, México, Imp. de José Batiza, 1870. 2 Vols.

———— *Memorias de un alférez*, Mérida, El Peninsular, 1904. 2 Vols.

Dávalos, Marcelino: *Carne de cañón*, México, Imp. del Museo Nacional de Arqueología, Historia y Etnología, 1915.

Díaz Covarrubias, Juan: *Gil Gómez el insurgente o la hija del médico*, in *Obras completas*. (The title page of the collection and the title of the first story are missing in the copy found in García Library. Another edition used was that of the *Biblioteca de Autores Mexicanos*, Vol. XLIII, México, Imp. de V. Agueros, 1902).

Don Juan de Escobar in *Biblioteca de Autores Mexicanos*, Vol. XXXIII, pp. 385-411.

Escosura, Patricio, de la: *La conjuración de México o los hijos de Hernán Cortés*, Madrid, 1850, México, 1850.

Fernández de Lizardi, José Joaquín: *La educación de las mujeres o la Quijotita y su prima*, México, Ballescá y Cía., 1897.

—————— *El Periquillo Sarniento*, Barcelona, Sopena, 1908.

Frías, Heriberto: *¿Áquila o sol?*, México, Imp. Franco-Mexicana, 1923.

—————— *Episodios militares mexicanos*, México and París, 1901. 2 Vols.

—————— *Leyendas históricas mexicanas*, México-Barcelona, Maucci, 1899.

—————— *Las miserias de México*, México, Botas, n. d.

—————— *Tomochic*, Barcelona, Maucci, 1899.

—————— *El triunfo de Sancho Panza*, México, Imp. de L. Herrera, 1911.

———— *El último duelo*, Mazatlán, 1907.

Gómez de Avellaneda, Gertrudis: *Guatimozín, último emperador de México*, Madrid, 1846; México, 1853, 1857.

Gómez de la Cortina: *La calle de don Juan Manuel*, in *Revista Mexicana*, México, I. Cumplido, 1835, pp. 551-560.

Jicoténcal, Philadelphia, Imp. de Guillermo Snavely, 1827. 2 Vols.

Lafragua, José María: *Netzula*, in *Biblioteca de Autores Mexicanos*, Vol. XXXIII, pp. 265-306.

Martínez de Castro, Manuel: *Eva*, México, Tip. lit. de Filomeno Mata, 1885. 3 Vols.

Mateos, Juan A.: *El Cerro de las Campanas*, México and Buenos Aires, Maucci, Novísima edición, n. d.

———— *Los insurgentes, continuación de Sacerdote y caudillo*, México, 1902.

———— *La majestad caída*, México, Maucci Hnos., n.d.

———— *Memorias de un guerrillero*, México, El Mundo, 1897. 2 Vols.

———— *Sacerdote y caudillo*, México and Buenos Aires, Maucci, Novísima edición, n. d.

———— *El sol de mayo,* México and Buenos Aires, Maucci, n. d.

Mejía, Demetrio: *Entre el amor y la patria,* México, La Voz de México, 1900.

Meléndez y Muñoz, Mariano: *El misterioso,* Guadalajara, 1836.

Navarro, Mariano: *Angela,* in *Biblioteca de Autores Mexicanos,* Vol. XXXIII, pp. 309-335.

Olavarría y Ferrari, Enrique: *Episodios nacionales mexicanos,* México and Paris, Parres, 1886-1887, 4 large Vols.

———— *El tálamo y la horca,* México, Díaz de León y White, 1868.

Pacheco, J. R.: *El criollo,* in *Biblioteca de Autores Mexicanos,* Vol. XXXIII, pp. 339-382.

Payno, Manuel: *Los bandidos de Río Frío,* México and Buenos Aires, Maucci, n. d. (This was probably printed during the latter part of 1927 and the first part of 1928).

———— *El fistol del diablo,* 3rd edition, Barcelona and Mexico, Parres y Cía., 1887. 2 Vols.

———— Several short historical stories found in

a collection called *Episodios históricos de la Guerra de Independencia,* México, 1910.

—————— *Tardes nubladas,* México, 1871.

Paz, Ireneo: *Amor y suplicio,* 7th edition, México, Imp. de Ireneo Paz, 1898.

—————— *Doña Marina,* México, Imp. de Ireneo Paz, 1883.

—————— *Leyendas históricas,* 2nd edition, México, Imp. de Ireneo Paz, 1885-1902. (Outside cover of the first volume has date 1894 and title page has 1886).

Pesado, José Joaquín: *El inquisidor de México,* in *Biblioteca de Autores Mexicanos,* Vol. XXXIII, pp. 3-46.

Pusalgas y Guerris, Ignacio Miguel: *El nigromántico mejicano.* Barcelona, 1838.

Riva Palacio, Vicente: *Calvario y Tabor,* edición León Sánchez, México, 1923.

—————— *Las dos empedradas,* México, Ballescá y Suc., 1909.

—————— *Martín Garatuza,* México, Imp. de La Constitución Social, 1868.

—————— *Memorias de un impostor,* México, M. C. de Villegas, 1872.

—————— *Monja y casada, virgen y mártir,*

México, Imp. de La Constitución Social, 1868.

———— *Los piratas del golfo*, México, Imp. de La Constitución Social, 1869.

———— *La vuelta de los muertos*, México, Díaz León y S. White, 1870.

Rodríguez Beltrán, Cayetano: *Pajarito*, México, Gómez de la Puente, 1908.

Rodríguez Galván: *La hija del oidor*, in *El año nuevo*, 1837, also in *Biblioteca de Autores Mexicanos*, Vol. XXXIII, pp. 91-114.

Salado Álvarez, Victoriano: *De Santa Anna a la Reforma, memorias de un veterano*, Barcelona, Henrich y Cía., México, J. Ballescá, 1902.

———— *La Intervención y el Imperio*, México, J. Ballescá, Suc., 1903-1906.

Sierra, Justo (padre): *Un año en el hospital de San Lázaro, Biblioteca de Autores Mexicanos*, Vol. LIV.

———— *La hija del judío, Biblioteca de Autores Mexicanos*, Vol. LXIII.

Sigüenza y Góngora, Carlos: *Los infortunios que Alonso Ramírez padeció, etc.* México, B. Calderón, 1690.

El visitador, in *Biblioteca de Autores Mexicanos,*
Vol. XXXIII, pp. 413-433,